EXPERIENCING GOD Outside *the* Box

In *Experiencing God Outside the Box*, Paul Meier, MD, challenges us to think outside the box of many Christian experiences. Tapping into a long ground breaking career in Christian Counseling and Psychiatry, Paul brings us face to face with many new facts and experiences that will hopefully enable us to re-think and "re-search" our relationship with God. Especially useful is how our childhood experiences directly affect our perception of our Heavenly Father. This book will certainly help many find a new and more intimate relationship with the "real God" and Father of us all.

—Esly Regina Carvalho, Ph.D.
Clinical Director, TraumaClinic do Brasil

"Our deepest need is to experience God as He truly is. Paul Meier gives us the complete picture of how to do this, spiritually, emotionally, relationally and neurologically. You will be a better person for reading this."

—John Townsend, Leadership Consultant, Psychologist
and co-author of the bestselling *Boundaries* series

EXPERIENCING
GOD
Outside *the* Box

Growing More Intimate
with the REAL GOD

Paul Meier, MD

NEW YORK

EXPERIENCING GOD Outside *the* Box
Growing More Intimate with the REAL GOD

Published in New York, New York, by Morgan James Faith. Morgan James and The Entrepreneurial Publisher are trademarks of Morgan James, LLC.
www.MorganJamesPublishing.com

The Morgan James Speakers Group can bring authors to your live event. For more information or to book an event visit The Morgan James Speakers Group at www.TheMorganJamesSpeakersGroup.com.

A **free** eBook edition is available with the purchase of this print book.

CLEARLY PRINT YOUR NAME ABOVE IN UPPER CASE

Instructions to claim your free eBook edition:
1. Download the BitLit app for Android or iOS
2. Write your name in **UPPER CASE** on the line
3. Use the BitLit app to submit a photo
4. Download your eBook to any device

ISBN 978-1-63047-387-7 paperback
ISBN 978-1-63047-388-4 eBook
ISBN 978-1-63047-389-1 hardcover
Library of Congress Control Number:
2014947420

Cover Design by:
Rachel Lopez
www.r2cdesign.com

Interior Design by:
Bonnie Bushman
bonnie@caboodlegraphics.com

In an effort to support local communities, raise awareness and funds, Morgan James Publishing donates a percentage of all book sales for the life of each book to Habitat for Humanity Peninsula and Greater Williamsburg.

Get involved today, visit
www.MorganJamesBuilds.com

Habitat for Humanity®
Peninsula and
Greater Williamsburg
Building Partner

Dedication

God has graciously blessed me with a wife who not only loves me and is devoted to me, but who loves God intimately—outside the box. I have been writing bits and pieces of this book for about eight years now, with much of it based on Jan's challenges for me to see God and his word outside the box. We pray together and serve God together and both have more questions than answers, but are grateful for the answers we have found. Thank you, Jan. I love you.

—Paul

Table of Contents

Foreword

This is an amazing book! It helped me see God in ways I never saw him before and to grow closer to him. It showed me many powerful ways to overcome the prejudices of my past. It will for sure influence your world-view and your God-view for your best. I highly recommend it to anyone who sincerely desires to understand who God is and how he interacts with us. Dr. Paul Meier is a powerful man of God, who has already changed the lives of millions of people all around the world. He knows God personally like nobody else I know. He is a man who lives a holy life with all his heart, day by day. I can tell that for sure as we are sharing emails on our faith-life almost every day for many years.

—**Dr. Jean-Luc Bertrand**, Paris, France
Author of 4 books, Emmy award TV producer winner for documentary on AIDS children, former CEO and owner of a major professional sports team in France, and Founder and CEO of Generation Africa, (www.generation-africa.org), an NGO that raises and trains more than 2000 orphans whose parents died of AIDS in South Africa.

Introduction

"My soul thirsts for God, for the living God. When can I go and meet with God?"

—King David (Psalm 42:2)

What is a psychiatrist doing writing a book about experiencing God outside the box? Thousands of our Meier Clinics clients eventually ask our 100+ psychiatrists, psychologists, and therapists spiritual questions that will be addressed in this book. If you have doubts and lots of unanswered questions about God, then, in my opinion, that makes the real God who created you very happy, because you are making good use of the heart and brain he gave you when he created you in his spiritual image.

To have no doubts or questions about God is to be spiritually lazy, because you have passively accepted whatever the authorities in your environment taught you, or you are assuming that your Heavenly Father is merely a grand photocopy of your earthly father, a mistake most people make to some extent. Even your genetic makeup and brain chemistry distort your view of God, of others, of yourself, and even of life itself. You think you have a personal relationship with the real God who created this expanding universe, and you may. But your relationship might very well be with a God In The Box, with many of the influences and pat answers you have been told and passively accepted without thinking it through.

Stop and think about this concept for a moment: If you ask seven billion strangers to tell you what they think the real God of this universe is really like, you will get some views of God that are similar, but each will be uniquely somewhat different. The fact that seven billion people have seven billion differing views of God proves that not a single one of them can be completely correct. Think about that, because that also proves that your view of God as well as my own view cannot possibly be 100 percent correct and our views are certainly not 100 percent comprehensive. We only know a small fraction of what we can know about him until we spend time with him in person in Heaven.

The purpose of this book is not to take away anyone's faith in God, but rather to assist you in the most noble and spiritually rewarding of all earthly tasks—experiencing God outside the box. This means seeing him more closely, in an accurate picture, after reading this book. It also means growing more intimate with God than you already are now while basing your relationship partially or largely on how you have been programmed to see him and know him.

(CHAPTER ONE)

The Father Factor

|--|

"Life can only be understood backwards; but it must be lived forwards."
—Søren Kierkegaard

Healing Father Wounds that Hinder
Our Ability to See God Outside the Box

W hen we are growing up and learning to say our "Goodnight Prayers," as three- or four- year-olds, we are actually thinking as we pray, "Dear Heavenly version of my earthly father." Research shows that nearly 80 percent of our God concept comes from our parent images, especially that of our earthly father. Every single one of us, as humans, is prejudiced to some degree toward (or against) God. We not only think our Heavenly Father is very much like our earthly father, we also try to avoid looking at painful repressed memories about our earthly fathers,

1

often holding them up on a pedestal to avoid getting in touch with our rage toward them, and displace this rage onto God instead, looking for reasons to reject God or at least keep him at a safe distance.

Case Study

Jim came to our Day Program after going through the divorce of his one and only marriage. He was very suicidal at the time, feeling hopeless, and feeling like God could never accept him—if there even is a God, which he doubted. People come to our Day Program to get seven hours a day, five days a week of intensive group and individual therapy, usually for about three weeks. We pack six months to a year of therapy into that three-week period, digging for root problems and using Gestalt and other techniques to get individuals in touch with their problems and repressed emotions.

We see each patient daily to make adjustments to their medications if meds are needed to relieve their intense anxiety, sadness, and insomnia. We also ask them about their childhoods and their dreams, which are often windows into their souls. Jim's individual therapist put an empty chair in front of Jim after we all learned about his childhood and subsequent encounters. Then the therapist had Jim pretend his father was sitting in the chair. Then he had Jim look his "father" in the eye and tell him how he felt about his father seldom being there for Jim, bringing up multiple specific incidents of feeling let down or downright rejected by his father. This is an example of a Gestalt technique to hasten recovery, rather than merely talking about his father.

Jim wept with grief and rage as he got in touch with his suppressed emotions. But then Jim prayed for God to enable him to forgive his father, so his life would no longer be haunted and unconsciously determined by his codependency on his father and father substitutes.

Jim was encouraged to build a few close male friends who could accept him as he is. As Jim saw the truth and forgave his father, and himself, it became much easier to develop an intimate friendship with his Heavenly

Father. Jim apologized to God for being so prejudiced against him, thinking him to be just like his father.

Jim recovered from his lifelong bouts of depression, continued in outpatient therapy for a few more months and continued to grow in his relationship with God. Eighteen months later, Jim fell in love with a wonderful woman from his church, dated her for a year, and then married her. He has now been happily married to her for three years and has a one-year-old son, a son he spends lots of time with and gives plenty of hugs to, knowing he, to some extent, represents what God is like to his own son.

The Psalm 103 Experiment

When I taught pastoral counseling at Trinity Evangelical Divinity School (Deerfield, Illinois, outside Chicago) in the 1970s, I conducted a research experiment to see if our father image really did prejudice our image of God the Heavenly Father. I took Psalm 103 and listed 13 of the attributes of God listed in that chapter (out of the 30 that are either stated or implied) and listed these attributes on a sheet of paper, with a space beside each trait to write down comments. I asked the students to only write down comments on the traits that they had trouble believing on a deep inner level, even if they agreed with the traits intellectually.

Each student, as would be expected, had his unique list of traits he struggled with, and some had few and some had many. When they were finished doing that, I gave them another similar sheet with the same 13 traits listed, but this time I asked them to write down comments beside the traits that were their own earthly fathers' weakest. They were shocked at the results. In almost every case, the doubts about God were identical to their own earthly fathers' weakest traits. These future pastors became aware of how they were allowing their own childhoods to prevent them from having a deeper and more intimate relationship with God. Their father images put God in a box for them—a box shaped like their earthly fathers. Becoming aware of this insight, as the readers of this book will as well, enabled them to see God more accurately, outside that box.

PSALM 103

¹ Praise the LORD, *my soul; all my inmost being, praise his holy name. ² Praise the* LORD, *my soul, and forget not all his benefits—³ who forgives all your sins and heals all your diseases, ⁴ who redeems your life from the pit and crowns you with love and compassion, ⁵ who satisfies your desires with good things so that your youth is renewed like the eagle's.*

⁶ The LORD *works righteousness and justice for all the oppressed. ⁷ He made known his ways to Moses, his deeds to the people of Israel: ⁸ The* LORD *is compassionate and gracious, slow to anger, abounding in love. ⁹ He will not always accuse, nor will he harbor his anger forever; ¹⁰ he does not treat us as our sins deserve or repay us according to our iniquities. ¹¹ For as high as the heavens are above the earth, so great is his love for those who fear him; ¹² as far as the east is from the west, so far has he removed our transgressions from us.*

¹³ As a father has compassion on his children, so the LORD *has compassion on those who fear him; ¹⁴ for he knows how we are formed, he remembers that we are dust. ¹⁵ The life of mortals is like grass, they flourish like a flower of the field; ¹⁶ the wind blows over it and it is gone, and its place remembers it no more. ¹⁷ But from everlasting to everlasting the* LORD's *love is with those who fear him, and his righteousness with their children's children—¹⁸ with those who keep his covenant and remember to obey his precepts.*

¹⁹ The LORD *has established his throne in heaven, and his kingdom rules over all.*

²⁰ Praise the LORD, *you his angels, you mighty ones who do his bidding, who obey his word. ²¹ Praise the* LORD, *all his heavenly hosts, you his servants who do his will. ²² Praise the* LORD, *all his works everywhere in his dominion. Praise the* LORD, *my soul.*

Psalm 103 Implies 30 Traits of God

1. Forgiving. Jesus said, "Father, forgive them, for they know not what they do (Luke 23:34-47)." We don't see our own unconscious motives without help. Jesus wanted the Father to forgive even those who had crucified him.
2. Healing.

3. Redeeming.

4. Honoring (Crowns Us). Two thousand years ago the Apostle Paul said the encouraging words to each of us, "You are God's masterpiece," despite our personal underestimations. "You are precious and honored in my sight … because I love you (Isaiah 43:4)." "The Lord takes delight in his people; he crowns the humble with salvation (Psalm 149:4)."

5. Loving (Abounding in Love).

6. Teaching. God even teaches us how to turn our personal failures into spiritual and emotional growth. Success is great, but sometimes we can make it harmful to our character, with our natural tendency toward narcissism. He teaches us how to turn our successes into growth also.

7. Compassionate. "The Lord is gracious and compassionate; slow to anger and rich in love (Psalm 145:8)."

8. Satisfying.

9. Giving Us Gifts and Blessings. When people have needs, God may purposely delay for their own good, but "in the proper season I will send the showers they need. There will be showers of blessing (Ezekiel 34:26)." God answers our prayers with yes, no or wait. The Apostle Paul promised (Philippians 4:19) that God would meet all the legitimate needs he determined would be best for us—not all our wants! There are some things we get special rewards for: "God blesses those who patiently endure testing and temptation (James 1:12)." Enduring testing and temptations means that, in Heaven, "we will receive the crown of life that God has promised (James 1:12)." We also are promised special rewards in Heaven for helping others find a relationship with God, and for yearning Christ's return to earth.

10. Renewing.

11. Righteous.

12. Just (Fair). "There is neither Jew nor Greek, there is neither bond nor free, there is neither male nor female: for ye are all one in Christ

Jesus (Galatians 3:28-29, KJV)." Jesus was not chauvinistic. His close pure friend, Mary Magdalene, was the last person he saw at his death and the first when he arose.

13. Protects Those Who Are Oppressed Or Abused. "Lord, we have waited for you. Be our strong arm each day and our salvation in times of trouble (Isaiah 33:2)."

14. Revealing Truth.

15. Goodness. Sometimes it feels as if God's rules keep us from a pleasurable life, but his purpose is to give us a good, rich, and satisfying life. (John 10:10)

16. Kindness. "I have loved you with an everlasting love; I have drawn you with loving-kindness (Jeremiah 31:3)."

17. Gracious. There are no sins whatsoever that will separate his children from his love. Ephesians 2:8-9 says "not of works" but only faith—grace.

18. Slow to Anger.

19. Not Accusatory.

20. Not Bitter.

21. Merciful.

22. Lenient (Does not give us the punishment we deserve).

23. Understanding.

24. Remembers Us.

25. Thinks About Us.

26. Omnipotent. "You are the God who does wonders; you have made known your strength among the peoples. By your arm you have redeemed us (Psalm 77:14-19)."

27. Omniscient. *"As heavens are higher than the earth, so are my ways higher than your ways, and my thoughts than your thoughts."* (Isaiah 55:8-9)

28. Omnipresent.

29. Ruling.

30. Desires Our Praise, Our Love, and Our Worship. God promises (Psalm 46:10) that we need not strive, because he will ultimately be

exalted in the nations. God desires for us to be happy, thankful, and to maintain an attitude of conversational prayer to him and from him daily (I Thessalonians 5:16-18).

Now I would like to ask you, the reader, to conduct this same experiment that my students did. Look at the 13 primary traits of God listed below and make comments beside each trait that gives you doubts about God. Then repeat it with which traits were your father's (or mother's) weakest.

1. Forgiving.
2. Healing.
3. Redeems Our Lives.
4. Loving.
5. Kind.
6. Satisfies Us With Good Things.
7. He Is Fair To Us.
8. He Pities Us So Is Merciful.
9. Gracious.
10. Slow To Anger.
11. He Understands Us.
12. He Keeps His Promises To Us.
13. He Rules Well.

(CHAPTER TWO)

Climbing 10 Mountains that Keep Us from Experiencing God Outside the Box

|———————————————————————————————|

1. The Father Factor

The father factor is perhaps the highest mountain to climb to experience God outside the box and was explained in Chapter One.

2. Rejection by Family and Peers

> *"Never expend energy obsessing about the past. The only direction is forward."*
>
> **—Jack Graham**

According to psychiatry research, about half of our basic adult personality patterns are laid down by our third birthday, and about 85 percent by our sixth birthday. How we look at men, women, ourselves, conflict, God, and life itself are all largely programmed into us.

Three things determine how we each turn out: our genes, our environment (especially early childhood), and our choices. We are not locked into the prejudices we have erroneously formed. But most people don't take the time or effort to become independent and learn to think for themselves. Most continue on in the same pattern their ancestors did before them.

Psychiatrists worry more about the totally compliant child who gets straight A's than the one who gets normal grades and rebels somewhat growing up. The latter is usually healthier mentally as an adult than the former totally compliant one. And when we are six years old, we tend to see ourselves through the eyes of our parents. If they respect and love and esteem us, we respect and love and esteem ourselves. If they treat us as though we were evil for thinking independently for ourselves, or stupid, or worthless, then we tend to see ourselves the same way. If they give us "don't exist" messages directly or indirectly, we become more prone toward suicide later in life. And our culture is deteriorating because God is being left out of the picture to a much greater extent than ever. That is one of the reasons why the teen suicide rate is 300 percent higher now than it was 50 years ago. Teens with a religious affiliation have a lower suicide rate.

We tend to overvalue parental acceptance of us. If you really stop and think about it, the truth is that there are seven billion people on planet earth, and your father is just one of them. Your mother is just one of them. Their opinion of you, in light of this, is practically irrelevant. We can all be "fathered and mothered" psychologically and spiritually by healthier individuals in our lives. Churches are great places for this to get facilitated.

Churches are great places to get fathered and mothered and brothered and sistered. Many people in this world—probably most—grow up in homes where they will face some pretty significant parental rejection if they think for themselves about who God really is and come to different conclusions from their parents. In some cultures, the children are literally murdered if they change faiths. In other cultures, they are treated as if they are dead. In others, they are rejected. In some, they are given the liberty to think for themselves and come to their own conclusions.

I believe it is good to teach our children all about our own faith in God and our perspectives of him, but to also listen to their thoughts and give them rope to come up with some differing conclusions. If you, as an adult now, believe what you believe about God just because of your fear of rejection by parents or your peers, then you are to be greatly pitied. It is better to learn and operate on the truth in your life, giving your life meaning and all the benefits of a deep relationship with the true God. It is better to experience eternal benefits than to believe a lie, or pretend like you believe a lie, just to get the conditional acceptance of a selfish parent who is merely one out of seven billion people on this planet.

Being your biological gene donors does not entitle your parents to rule over you when you become an adult. The Bible says little children should obey their parents, not adult children (Ephesians 6:1 in the original Greek). Jesus said that unless you hate your father and mother in comparison to your love for him, you are unworthy to be called his disciple (Luke 14:26).

3. Fear of Having to Give up Pet Sins

It seems to me, as a psychiatrist, that many people decide what sins they want to commit, and then find a religion that will back them up! We fear daily meditation on Scripture because it will certainly eventually convict us of sinful thoughts and behaviors and motives that we were not aware of until then. As a teenager, I wrote in the back of my Bible, "This Book (the Bible) will keep you from sin. Sin will keep you from this Book."

4. Bitterness

Almost every one of us, at one time or another, becomes bitter toward God for not living up to our expectations of him. As we stated earlier, bitterness toward our earthly father or mother can also get transferred erroneously (projected) unto our Heavenly Father. In Ephesians 4:26-27 we are told that it is fine to get angry and that we can get angry without sinning, but if we hold on to bitterness, we give Satan a foothold in our lives.

Bitterness destroys us. It is the leading cause of death because it causes such horrible biochemical changes within our brains and bodies.

We even have fewer antibodies to ward off diseases. It is the leading cause of depression and suicides. Bitterness drives us away from an intimate relationship with God. We hang on to bitterness because of an unconscious or conscious need to get personal vengeance on someone—perhaps even on God or ourselves.

We are told in Romans 12 to turn all vengeance over to God and give it up in our own lives, because God promises to repay in his own time and in his own way. God knows our hearts. He knows the heart of the person who harmed you or abused you. And God will judge and punish him accordingly. In Psalm 68 we read that God loves widows and orphans, and I believe that includes psychological widows and orphans. He will smash the heads of their abusers against the rocks unless they truly and sincerely, in the depths of their hearts, repent of their horrible deeds. Don't allow any form of bitterness to keep you from experiencing intimacy with God outside the box. I love hearing the Rolling Stones song, "You Don't Always Get What You Want," then remind myself that God always gives us what we need (Philippians 4:13).

5. Hypocrites in the Church

There are hypocrites in almost every church, of course, because there are hypocrites almost everywhere. I get hungry for food for the nourishment of my body, so I go to the grocery store. There are as many hypocrites in a typical grocery store as there are in a typical church, but that doesn't keep me from going to the store to purchase food for my physical nourishment. Some grocery stores have very healthy foods, while others have unhealthy foods. In the same way, there are spiritually healthy churches and spiritually unhealthy churches. I need spiritual nourishment for my soul as much or more than I need physical nourishment for my body. I get spiritual nourishment from many places—the Holy Spirit, friends, circumstances, experiences, meditation, Bible study, prayer, and also churches. I go to the mentally and spiritually healthiest churches I can find for spiritual food, like seeking a healthy grocery store for physical food. After all, God calls us to soar with the eagles, not to be gobbled up by turkeys!

6. Creation, Noah's Ark, and the Miracles

My wife and I recently saw a film about Noah's Ark in which enormous adult elephants, giraffes, and hundreds of species of snakes were all getting on board. How absurd. I believe the Noah's Ark story. I risked my own life to be the team physician for astronaut Jim Irwin's mountain climbing expedition up Mount Ararat in 1985.

Jim Irwin wanted to prove the existence of Noah's Ark above the Ahora Gorge at the 16,500-foot level, where photos that were classified at that time showed it may very well be buried in the ice. Our team was caught by terrorists on the mountain who burned all our equipment, lined my team up in a firing squad to shoot us but changed their minds, and chased my team down the mountain. The terrorists were found and killed on the spot the next day by Turkish soldiers.

There are possibly a thousand or more species evolving daily in our world, and a thousand or more becoming extinct daily. It is all usually a good thing. It is part of the natural selection process—the survival of the fittest. These species fit into genuses of animals, a much smaller group, and then families of animals, like the family of dog-type animals, and then kinds of animals, like mammals.

Thousands of years ago, according to recent genetic research, wolves may have evolved into all the other types of animals in the dog family. Noah's Ark may have just had two baby wolves to evolve into all the other doglike animals. If elephants were on board, they were baby elephants, not adults. But there were enough "types" or "kinds" of animals on board to evolve into the millions of species we see today, based on natural selection and survival of the fittest in each environment.

And as far as miracles, I have witnessed what I consider in the realm of the miraculous and will share some of these stories in this book. I have never witnessed numerous miracles Jesus performed during his public ministry on earth 2,000 years ago, like watching a crippled man's crooked bones all getting straightened out and his muscles instantly restored as he took up from his bed and walked. But just because I have never seen some of them does not prove that they have not occurred.

There are devout Christians on all sides of the creation vs. evolution conflict. Whatever I would find out to be true does not in the least hinder me from experiencing God outside the box. I am also a scientist who has published scientific articles, but I believe in a literal seven-day creation personally, but also that the earth is billions of years old and was without form and void until God chose to do his acts of creation on it. Why not? God can do anything. If I am wrong about seven literal days, so what?

Some believe each day represents a period of time. Some believe in Darwinian ape-to-man type evolution, guided by God, called theistic evolution. These are all our brothers who love Jesus but have differences of opinions. I hope they accept me in spite of my literal opinion as easily as I accept them. But I beg you, please, do not let Noah's Ark, miracles or creationism opinions keep you from developing intimacy with the real God.

7. Mother Nature versus God

It is popular nowadays, especially among some of the popular movie stars and naive people who idolize them, to go around hugging trees and worshipping Mother Nature. But God said in Romans 1 that studying nature draws us closer to God, not further away. Einstein, upon learning more and more of the natural laws that rule the entire universe, came to the personal conclusion that there has to be a God. A design implies a designer.

When I studied the human body in medical school and the human mind at Duke University Psychiatry Residency, I grew closer to God, not further away. The human body has 30 trillion cells, each cell with thousands of enzymes, endoplasmic reticulum, golgi apparatuses; trillions of electrons, protons, and neutrons, etcetera. If you took just one of those 30 trillion cells and blew it up the size of a cathedral, it would have trillions of parts, and if you took even one atom out of those trillions from the one cell and blew it up the size of a cathedral, only God knows what you would see in that atom.

If you take one enzyme out of those 30 trillion cells, the body would die. To honestly think that our complex bodies came about without a God is like saying Webster's Dictionary came about as a result of an explosion in a printing factory with all the words and letters falling together into place. It is absurd.

Atheism takes a million times more faith than believing in a Creator does. In fact, when I treat atheists, I won't initially talk to them about God. Depending on their family history, I usually get them to focus on their conflicts toward their absent or abusive fathers. When they resolve their father conflicts, they often develop an intimate relationship with God on their own. It is not always like that, but quite commonly their father image determines their atheism. Have you ever noticed that most reasonable Christians love atheistic neighbors as individuals, regardless of their atheism, but so many atheists are hostile and bitter toward Christians and Christianity? Many of them got burned out from legalistic and unhealthy Christian homes and parents, so rebel against God altogether now.

8. What Will It Cost Me?

If you decide to become a Christian in order to guarantee a peaceful and trouble-free life, forget it. Becoming a Christian does bring more joy and meaning into your life, but it also brings trials and tribulations. Job was a godly man who suffered horrible skin disease and pain, and who lost his children. His erroneous wife and friends told him it must be due to his sins, but it was not his fault at all. Job replied to his wife, "What? Shall we expect good from God and not also expect adversity (Job 2:10)?" The Apostle Paul totally dedicated his life to God and as a result was beaten almost to death twice, shipwrecked three times, and died in prison, but he died happy and thanking God for the honor of suffering for God. "Pain is God's megaphone to rouse a deaf world," C.S. Lewis so wisely exclaimed.

9. The Rat Race

There are seven billion people out here on planet earth, and all seven billion of us, to one extent or another, go through life feeling like a nobody and trying to prove to those around us (and to ourselves) that we are not a nobody. We do this primarily through sex, money, and power—the lust of the flesh, the lust of the eyes, and the pride of life. We waste our lives trying and failing to live up to the Joneses. And even if we beat the Joneses, we still feel just as empty and meaningless on a deep inner level. We still have angst. It is only by purposely withdrawing from the rat race and devoting our lives instead to developing a deep, intimate relationship to the one true God, out of the box, and seeking his will for our lives, that our lives take on meaning and we learn to love and be loved in ways like he loves and is loved.

10. Fear of Thinking about Death and Eternity

Most people seem to me to not like funerals. Not only do you grieve the loss of a loved one, at least until you join him or her again someday in Heaven, but funerals also remind us of our own mortality. Most people don't like to think about death. I remember asking a friend what kind of life insurance he had set up for his family for after his death. I was shocked to hear my friend say, "I'm not going to die! I'll set that up when I get old." He was actually angry with me, without really saying so, for asking him something that related to his mortality.

I may die in 30 years or in 30 minutes or in 30 seconds. Only God knows. I think it is a good idea to think once in a while about our own mortality. The Bible says in many places that we are like a blade of grass or a flower that springs up, blossoms, then withers and dies. Our life on earth is very short compared to eternity. If eternity were a trillion-mile-long road, your life on earth would be the length of a pinhead. Actually much less. Thinking about God and meditating on Scripture forces us to face our mortality, and that is enough to keep some people from developing a deep relationship with the real God outside the box. Please don't let it hinder you. Preparing for death actually makes your life better and more focused on the true gold of love rather than the false gold of sex, money, and power.

This book will introduce you to many new concepts that will give all of our reading family more insight into our flawed thinking and decision-making patterns, whether the reader be atheist, Muslim, Jew, Hindu, New Age, or Christian. It will change your life for the better or else I have completely failed in my genuine desire to make a contribution to your life—the dream of every good but God-centered psychiatrist.

Many years ago, I remember being fascinated by a TV show in which there would be a guest panel and then three people would come out on stage and all would claim to be the same person with the same name (like Jack Smith) and same career, etcetera. After all the panelists got to ask their own questions about the lives of each of the three people, with one of those three always telling the truth and the other two always lying and making something up, then the panel would vote on who they thought was the real Jack Smith. The host of the show would then say in a loud, deep voice, "Will the real Jack Smith please stand up?" When the real Jack Smith did stand up, it would often not be the one the panel thought it would be.

I have often wondered what it would be like to have a repeat of that show, but have the real God and two fake gods show up, with all of you who are currently reading this book and myself on the panel. When the TV host yells out, "Will the real God please stand up," would we guess the right one?

Being a psychiatrist and hearing my clients describing their views of God differently, I really doubt that many of us would guess the right one. We all see God in a box to some extent or another.

What denomination perfectly portrays the real God, by the way? Is it Catholic, Baptist, Church of Christ, Nazarene, Pentecostal, Presbyterian, Methodist, Muslim, Hindu, Seventh Day Adventist, Lutheran, Greek Orthodox, Episcopal, or what? My advice as a Christian psychiatrist is that if you belong to any denomination that thinks it has a lock on the truth, and that denomination is the only one that is right, get out of it as quick as you can. The Real God loves the humble, but resists the proud.

John the Baptist was Jesus's cousin. He grew up with Jesus. He knew Jesus was God in the flesh. He had more proof than you or I could ever dream of, even witnessing the miracles of Jesus firsthand. And yet, when John the Baptist (by the way, was he Southern Baptist, American Baptist, or Independent Baptist?) was in prison, getting ready to have his head cut off for confronting Herod about his sins, he wrote a little note to his cousin, Jesus. "Are you sure you are the one?" John asked. Jesus sent a reply back to John something like, "Well, you have seen me heal the sick, make paralyzed people walk, make blind people see, and even raise the dead back to life. Who do you think I am?"

John was satisfied and got over his personal doubts about God, even though he knew God personally through Jesus, and went ahead and got his head cut off rather than apologize to Herod. So if Jesus's own cousin had doubts about God, don't you think it must be rather normal for you and I, who have not seen all those things, to have doubts also? Of course it is! And I pity the denomination that thinks they have all the right pat answers or that they are the only ones righteous enough (they are committing the horrible sin of arrogant self-righteousness), when even John the Baptist had doubts.

Who is the real God? What is God really like? How do I really know what he is like? How do I know for sure that he even exists? How does his existence affect me and my lifestyle? Will he cramp my lifestyle? Is he someone I am afraid to get angry at me, because he might curse me in some way? Is he like a genie in the sky that I can use and manipulate to get the things (and people) that I want to own or control? If there really is a God, why did he let me get hurt so badly by so many people? Why can't I count on him to protect me from diseases, "bad luck," and dangerous people? Do some people really have a close relationship with God? Do they really hear him give them a sense of direction in their spirits somehow and hear him warn them about other situations somehow? Or are those people that claim that simply naive?

Was Sigmund Freud right more than 100 years ago when he said that there is no God? Was he right when he said that religion is the universal neurosis of mankind and that all of his patients who talked about God were really talking about a projected image of their fathers?

Being a psychiatrist myself, I have been asked all of the above questions thousands of times in the past 40 years of private practice. Naive people from various church denominations spout off pat answers that they learned in sermons or indoctrination classes. Most people are so passive they spend the rest of their lives parroting back whatever they have learned about God without even questioning whether what they have learned has any basis in reality whatsoever.

The purpose of this book is to help all of us (myself included) who have been so naive in the past that we thought we knew all the answers about God. Maybe it is time to grow up and become wise enough and humble enough to realize and admit that there are really a lot more questions than there are answers when it comes to really having a personal relationship with the true Spirit being called "God."

When you finish reading this book, it will change the rest of your life, no matter who you are when you start it, or else I have been an utter failure. Even if you, like Freud, were an atheist when you started this book and remain one after you finish it, this book will still change your life, because you will understand yourself much better. Good journey.

I would be the most arrogant person on planet earth if I told you I knew all the correct answers to the above questions. I merely want to share with you my own thoughts and doubts and personal guesses in order to stretch your imagination. So why would you give a rip about my opinions anyway? Why wouldn't reading my opinions be a total waste of time? Some of you will decide right this moment that it is a waste, so you will put the book down and never go back to it again, being totally satisfied with all the conclusions you have already made about God and willing to gamble the rest of your life, and—if the Bible is true—even gamble your eternal life on what you think you already know.

Well, here are some reasons why I think it will be worth your time and effort to read and think about my observations and opinions in this book:

1. I am a Duke-educated psychiatrist with 40 years of experience tying together what my patients say about God with what their earthly "gods"—their moms and dads—were like. I understand where Freud was coming from because I have had similar observations that he had more than 100 years ago, but with differing conclusions.

2. I have had 26 years of full-time education including a BS in biology, an MS in physiology, an MD in general medicine, a residency diploma from Duke in psychiatry, followed by ten more years of part-time graduate studies in theology and biblical studies at

Trinity Evangelical Divinity School in the Chicago area and Dallas Theological Seminary, where I taught full time on the faculty for 12 years and finally obtained my own seminary degree at age 40.

3. I have authored or coauthored more than 90 bestselling books on various aspects of the body, soul, and spirit. These books have sold nearly eight million copies in more than 30 languages.

4. I have lectured on the integration of the physical, biochemical, psychological, and spiritual aspects of man in many countries around the world, including Cuba, Peru, Turkey, Jordan, Israel (five different years), France, Germany, Sweden, Denmark, Norway, Mexico, Peru, and many others.

5. My mother was a third-grade educated but wise woman, and my dad was a carpenter, so I didn't start out life with any kind of super intellectual mentality. I actually believe my very simple beginnings are an asset, not a liability, when it comes to searching for truth without getting hung up by anyone's private predispositions. Rules are suggestions to me, unless they are clearly from God. I have been a lifelong skeptic and plan to stay that way. I have, since early infancy, kept asking questions about people and God and why we do what we do and think what we think. I know I drove some of my teachers nuts by constantly asking them question after question when they taught us things that the other kids simply memorized and parroted back to them on tests and quizzes. My 95-year-old German mother (now deceased) told me that when I was five years old, I was playing in the snow in our front yard when the neighborhood bully came walking by and belligerently pushed me down in the snow, then walked off. Rather than cry like most of my friends would have, I merely got up, brushed myself off, and walked contemplatively over to my mother, who was on the front porch watching all this. Then I asked, "Mom, I wonder why he did that?" I realized at age five that it must be some anger problem that the bully had from his home life or something.

6. I decided at age six that knowing the real God in a personal way was always going to be the most important priority in my life. My parents read the Bible to me and my three siblings every night since I was born, and at age ten, I decided to start reading and meditating on the Bible every day of my life, which I have done almost every day ever since with very few exceptions.

7. And finally, while trying to apply the scientific method to spirituality in graduate school, where I was an "Alumni Distinguished Graduate Fellow" at Michigan State University in the late 1960s, I tried very hard to ditch my Christian beliefs altogether. But after studying all the different religions and their own "bibles," and studying fulfilled prophecies in the Judeo/Christian bibles, I came to the conclusion that my Bible really was the correct one, and that the God described in that Bible was also the real God who created the universe billions of years ago. But if you are an atheist, or a Muslim, or Hindu, or Buddhist, or a New Ager, I really hope that nothing I say in the rest of this book will offend you in any way. I love you all and hope all of you learn more about yourselves from this book and gain many insights into how all of us humans develop flawed thinking. We are all a lot more primitive and naive and prejudiced than we could possibly ever imagine. I hope and pray that this book will help all of us to gain knowledge and skills that will better equip us to accomplish the most noble of all earthly tasks—experiencing God outside the box.

CHAPTER THREE

Codependency and Our View of God

Y ears ago my patient Kate was a rich, smart, beautiful movie star in her 30s, depressed from going through divorce number seven from abusive husbands. All seven husbands were drug or alcohol abusers who ran around on her often and beat her if she griped! She thought each one to be great at first. She told me she thought that "either all men are alike" or she "had extremely bad luck." I told her neither was true.

She had not shared with me yet anything about her childhood, so I asked her if I could guess her childhood based on her life. She allowed me to, then got angry and temporarily "fired me" when I guessed it all right. I had correctly guessed that the movie star's dad was an alcoholic who beat Kate's mom and repeatedly sexually abused Kate growing up. I told her that her unconscious was running her life, not her own conscious mind. I told her she was unconsciously repeating her childhood over and over again, like most of us do to one extent or another.

She did not want to accept that she had any role in causing all the horrible pain her life's path had led her down, in spite of all her beauty, fame, and money. That is why she initially fired me rather than accept the truth. But when the truth sunk in, she came back and "rehired" me. Her unconscious was trying to fix her childhood. She unconsciously wanted to marry someone like her father and change him into a good person. She wanted to be genuinely loved by someone like her father to fill the father-vacuum that dominated her life. She also wanted to get vengeance on her father and would unconsciously do so through her husbands. But she had blinders on and really thought her seven husbands were really nice guys at each wedding. So when she and each husband first met, there were six people present: the two as they saw themselves, the two as they very blindly saw each other, and the two as they really were—as only God sees them. Her husbands were addicted to alcohol, drugs, and sexual infidelity, but she was addicted to sociopaths of that particular "flavor." Her addiction is called "codependency."

Codependency was a relatively new word and unfamiliar concept in the late 1980s when I coauthored a book on it, *Love Is a Choice*. I was a guest on *The Oprah Winfrey Show* to discuss it, and it has since sold well more than a million copies and continues to be sold and read by thousands annually. We all have some of these codependency tendencies, and it influences every aspect of our lives, even our ability to see God outside the box.

I'm a Duke-educated psychiatrist (also an ordained minister) who weeps for those who suffer in any way, but making people dependent is cruel. An obsessive man counted all the verses in the Bible one time to find the middle one: "Put not your trust in man (Psalm 146:3)." Trust must be earned, not given. You can give someone love, but give no man trust because trust has to be earned over a long period of time.

Don't make yourself dependent on someone you cannot even trust yet, whether he is deemed trustworthy or not. Anyone who gets angry with you for not trusting him is especially untrustworthy. It is manipulation using shaming and false guilt. A wise and humble man would urge you not to trust him until he has proven himself trustworthy to you personally.

Trust must be earned based on actions, not words. My dad taught me as a youth, "Don't trust anyone until you have shared a bushel of salt," meaning so many meals together to use that much, figuratively speaking. Unhealthy families have four rules:

1. Don't talk (about true and important things).
2. Don't feel (talk about superficial things but not true feelings).
3. Don't trust anyone (except for blind trust of the dominant parent).
4. Always make the family look good (fake it in public).

Is it any wonder we learn at a young age to be blind to who we really are? When we are vulnerable and show the truth about who we really are, we are punished or rejected and learn to become phony, even with ourselves. At age three, we are nearly all "emotional geniuses"—in touch with our feelings. When we were angry, we expressed it. When we were sad, we cried. When we felt love, we hugged our mothers. But in sick codependent families, we learn it is not safe to express our true feelings, so we quit doing so, and soon even quit being aware of what emotions we are experiencing, or at least to what extent we are feeling them.

We become emotionally handicapped. But no matter how old we are, we can relearn to get in touch with and share true feelings, but often requiring intensive therapy. Three weeks in our Day Programs (seven hours a day of therapy, five days a week for an average of three weeks) usually succeeds in accomplishing this valuable goal of getting reaware of and expressing true feelings.

There is such a thing as healthy interdependence on others. Feeling like we can do everything ourselves without help from others is not healthy or biblical. But codependency is either when we do things for others that they would be better off doing themselves or depending on others to do things for you that you should be doing yourself. We can even be codependent with God. An example would be if you were lost at sea in a rowboat and suddenly saw shore in the great distance. Would you pray to God to float you there or would you row to shore. Either answer is the wrong one. The right answer is to pray to God and row to shore, depending on his strength and protection and guidance to get you there. That would be healthy interdependence.

Another example is when you develop a disease or become aware of a chemical deficiency in any organ of your body, including your brain, requiring a lifelong antidepressant. Would you insist that God correct it without taking the meds or going to a psychiatrist, or would you go straight to the psychiatrist for the meds and not pray to God for guidance? Again, the answer would be to pray to God for possible healing (never guaranteed—everyone Jesus ever healed on earth died of something else later!). Then pray for wisdom to find the best psychiatrist available in the meantime to get on the right meds.

Your brain, for example, runs on a chemical called serotonin, just like your car runs on gasoline. If your car ran out of gas, would you coast to the side of the road and then pray, "Dear Heavenly Father, please make my car run without gasoline from now on?" Could God do that? Of course he could! He is God. But would he do that? I doubt it. He would be spoiling you, making you think you are entitled to special privileges not given to other human beings. He would be making a narcissist out of you. He would probably tell you to get off your rear and go get your own gasoline at the nearest gas station or to call AAA or a friend. That is healthy interdependence on God rather than codependence.

What is scary is that every single one of us has many blind spots and areas of codependency. We project our unconscious faults on loved ones. Fathers tend to project on the oldest son more so than his other children, and moms on the oldest daughter, making the oldest child of each sex generally more perfectionistic and self-critical later. They may get better grades, go further in their education, and become more successful than their siblings as a result, but they generally enjoy life less than their siblings because they never feel quite good enough to please the critical parent residing in their brains now.

The cure is to become aware of these tendencies and to get to know the God of grace and unconditional love, then to practice being gracious with themselves. The cure is to find God's light and easy yoke and quit trying to please their imaginary demanding God who expects too much out of them. The fact that you are reading this type of book right now makes it more likely that you may very well fit into this category yourself, because perfectionists want to know everything, so are more likely to read informative books.

You can take what you just learned about yourself right now and make "redecisions" (new decisions) about the direction of your life in a more healthy direction. You may even be in the wrong career either to please a controlling parent or to rebel against the controlling parent. It would be healthier to decide what you love and are gifted at, and then find a career you enjoy in that field. Only 20 percent of adults in the United States, according to polls, enjoy their career. Eighty percent feel stuck in a career they do not enjoy. I know of a young man whose father demanded that he grow up to be a businessman and to get his MBA degree, even though that is not what the young teen wanted to do. As a young adult, he became a businessman and got all the way through MBA schooling except for one five-page paper needed to finish a course and graduate. He kept intending to do it, but kept putting it off. He was given a five-year extension to get it done, but never got his degree because he could not get himself to do what his father demanded, even though it would have meant an enormous pay increase. He continued being a businessman, however, even though he hated doing so. He was codependent and self-defeating. He had a failure script. And he did fail in business later.

Do you really think it is a coincidence that 15 of the first 16 astronauts were firstborn? They were great people but perfectionistic. How else would they make it to the moon and back? I knew three astronauts—two men and one woman. As I mentioned previously, I was the team physician for Jim Irwin's Mount Ararat expedition in 1985. Suni Williams is the female astronaut who spent the most time in space. After months in the space station, her perspective on our world matured even more. Suni Williams told me (back on earth!), that from space, she saw no national boundary lines—

just a big, beautiful planet for us to share. Being in space looking down at earth for months made Suni Williams wonder why humans foolishly kill each other over so many stupid things like religious prejudices. She told me that it matured her perspective on life and on God's creativity.

Our prejudices are not only toward God and others, but also toward ourselves. There is nothing wrong with loving the country you live in (known as patriotism), but at the same time it helps to see ourselves as eternal beings who will spend forever with other believers in Heaven, so we are mere sojourners and visitors here on planet earth.

I got degrees from five schools, including three who have good sports teams: Michigan State, Arkansas, and Duke. When I watch these teams play sports in championship games, I see myself through the eyes of a dedicated fan. One year all three of them were in the final eight in an NCAA tournament I took my son to, and two of them played for the national championship. I found my loyalties competing in my head to decide who to pull for. Again, that is fine, but not if that is my primary identity. My primary identity is not as a graduate of one of my five colleges, or even as an American (which I am proud to be), but as an eternal citizen of Heaven in an eternal loyal relationship with God.

I need to discover my true identity to have an honest and intimate relationship with God. The Apostle John said (John 8:32) that if we learn the truth, then the truth will set us free. Understanding why we commit certain sins helps us avoid them. It was also the Apostle John who said that if we say we no longer sin, we deceive ourselves. Again, we confess, learn, and go on with life. And, of course, the worst sinners (Proverbs 6) are those who proudly and arrogantly look down on other normal humans who sin— known as a "proud look."

If we are codependent we will put others down and dominate them to feel falsely and very temporarily better about ourselves, or we will be so dependent and beaten down that we get ourselves in situations where we are dominated and criticized by others. We will be addicted to abuse. Our healthy goal, again, is healthy interdependence with other healthy human beings, avoiding deeper relationships with the unhealthy as much as possible.

If someone is hungry, you could either make him dependent on you by taking him fish to eat every day, the codependent approach, or you can take him some fish temporarily but give him a fishing pole and teach him how to fish so he can feed himself from then on, the healthy interdependent way. Unhealthy codependency includes feeding or supporting anyone who can work but refuses. I Thessalonians 3:10 says those who refuse to work shouldn't eat.

And the ultimate question is whether we have an unhealthy, codependent God-view and worldview or a healthy interdependent relationship? A healthy relationship with the true Creator-God outside the box would include realizing how powerless we are without him, while seeking to do all he calls us to do in his power. Depending on God to do for us what he expects us to do for ourselves is a sick relationship with God. Then we get angry at him for letting us fall flat on our faces when we do so.

Doing more good deeds than he calls us to do with his light burden and easy yoke, in order to obey your confused notion of God, thinking he is like your demanding parent, is also spiritual codependency and unhealthy. It seems strange to realize we can actually do too many good deeds. If those excessive good deeds take us away from the relationship God wants us to have with our own families, then we are sinning even more by avoiding the most important callings in our lives.

Our bodies are the temples of the Holy Spirit, so God also wants us to take care of his temples. If we stay up until midnight doing "the Lord's work," then wake up at five a.m. every morning for prayer and Bible study, we are sinning against God by doing so. Our bodies need more than five hours a night of sleep to maintain good physical and mental health. Ignoring prayer and Bible meditation would be a big mistake spiritually as well. A healthy and mature believer will take time for enough sleep, time with family and friends, fun and relaxation, work, and also having quality time with God in meditation and prayer. It will take eliminating some things in his life, even valuable things sometimes, to get life in balance. But that is what God wants. And we need a healthy spiritual life to have a healthy physical and emotional life. The quest to deeply know the true God outside the box is a day by day attempt to balance our total dependence on God with the carrying out of our responsibilities to God and significant others in our lives.

CHAPTER FOUR

Oh, Death, Where is Thy Sting?

|—————————————————————————————————|

"Grant now such sweet communion with you as I read your word that if I hear of my impending death I will not be disappointed."

—John Piper

"O death, where is thy sting?" (KJV)

—The Apostle Paul (1 Corinthians 15:55)

"When you come to Jesus, you'll not only know how to live, you'll know how to die."

—Max Lucado

"Nails didn't hold God to a cross. Love did. The sinless One took on the face of a sinner so that we could take on the face of a saint!"

Scott Smith (KLOVE host)

"Because He lives we can face tomorrow, we have faith, hope and love and we have the gift of eternal life!"

A.W. Tozer

I f you have recently lost a loved one, I wish you good mourning. Grieve your loss, and weep over your loss. That is godly. But also get the death of your loved one in perspective. Look at how God views that death: "Blessed unto the Lord are the death of his saints (Psalm 116:16)." Everyone Jesus ever healed during his public ministry died of something else later. Death is an important part of life.

If we die of old age someday, do we want to face God leaving lots of things behind, dying alone and lonely, or die with loved ones by our side or even holding us? When my godly maternal grandfather died, my mom and my aunt were at his bedside holding his hand.

My grandfather had been rocking in his rocking chair, reading his Bible and singing a hymn to himself. I was a preteen, sitting beside my grandfather and enjoying his loving presence. Then he stopped and asked for my mom and her sister, my Aunt Pauline. He told them it was time for him to die and go to Heaven, so he got up and led them to his bedroom.

I started to follow him, but he told me to stay behind on his rocking chair. I remember feeling left out, but he must have thought I was too young to witness what was about to transpire. He lay down on his bed, and then looked up at the ceiling as though he saw something there (and I believe he did). He lifted up his right hand and pointed at the ceiling and had a big smile on his face, and then his hand dropped and he passed away.

My mom and aunt gave me all the details I had sadly missed out on. This happened in Saginaw, Michigan, and several states away, in Kansas, one of my grandpa's sons died at about the same time of a heart attack while singing a solo at his friend's funeral. But I will always remember that my grandpa looked up, pointed at the ceiling, dying with a smile.

When my father was almost 85 years old, he was still in great health, even climbing up on his roof to nail on some loose shingles and mowing his own lawn, refusing to allow me to hire someone to do so. But his aorta ruptured, and he was rushed by ambulance to the hospital, but it was too late to operate to save his life. The doctor told my dad and me that he would die within two or three days from the chemical buildup of toxic chemicals from the parts of his body that had already died.

Being an MD myself, I got to stay with my dad in intensive care, and wanted to be sure to be with him when he died. I had missed out on being with my grandpa and did not want to miss out on being with my own father. I could tell by looking at the monitor above his head that he was close to death, so my sister and I said our goodbyes to him and thanked him for being such a great dad.

We sang a hymn to him. Then I joked with him about not being allowed into Heaven until he went to a special room to learn how to dance first, since he never learned how. He laughed and was at peace about dying. I asked him if he was ready to die, and he said that he was. Then he looked quickly up at the ceiling somewhat startled, with a big smile appearing on his face, and his head dropped into my hands as he passed from this life to the next. It had been very similar to the way my maternal grandpa had died many years earlier. My sister and I wept with sadness for losing him but joy for what we had just witnessed and for the blessings we knew our dad was already receiving in Heaven.

When my godly mother was dying, she said she looked forward to joining my dad in Heaven and smiled, whispering, "I love you, Paul" with her last breath. My mom had three dreams the three nights before she died. In the first one, she dreamed that my dad came down from Heaven in the 1957 aqua-and-white Chevy he loved so much on earth, rather than in a chariot, to get my mom and fly her to Heaven.

Two nights before she died, she dreamed that her mom and dad were waiting for her when she got to Heaven. And the night before she died she dreamed that all her friends who had already died were waiting for her with a big party to celebrate her coming to join them.

My mom was nearly 97 when she passed away, and had been in good health just a week before. She got a routine physical exam and her blood drawn for routine lab tests. When the tests came back, her doctor could tell that her kidneys were starting to fail, so he called me up and told me my mom would very soon experience kidney failure and probably be gone within a matter of about four or five days.

I immediately left my own medical (psychiatric) office and drove to her room at her assisted living facility. I told her lovingly but frankly what the doctor had just told me, and that she would likely die within four or five days. Her reply to me was, "I hope the doctor was right, Paul. I'm almost 97, and I am ready to go and join your dad and my friends. I won't have arthritis or aches and pains in Heaven either."

I was pleasantly surprised by her very honest and matter-of-fact answer. I was expecting her to weep with sorrow, but she was all smiles. Then she immediately grabbed her telephone and started calling her grandchildren one at a time. I heard her tell each one that she was going home to Heaven soon and she wanted to say goodbye. She also wanted to be sure she saw each of them there someday, asking them for reassurance of their faith in God.

A month or so earlier, while she was still in very good health, I had been with her when she recorded her own two-minute funeral sermonette, encouraging those who would attend to have a relationship with God because it was so wonderful to face death knowing she knew where she was going. We played her sermonette at the funeral.

Six weeks or so before my mom got sick, I had one of my "God-dreams"—dreams that Jesus appears in. In this one my mom had just died and gone to Heaven, where she was dancing with my father. I was on earth in the dream, but could watch them in Heaven somehow. I yelled up to my mom to ask her if I could come up there and join them—to dance with my mother and father.

My mom replied, "Not just yet, my son. Your time will come soon enough. But remember all the love you received throughout your life from your family and share that love with the world by dancing with the world." All of these words and happenings were said as part of a four-minute long song I heard completely from start to finish with poetic words and a beautiful tune. I called the song "Dancing with Mother."

Being a musician myself, as soon as I awakened from the dream I rushed and grabbed a pen and paper and jotted down the words and tune of the song. I sent it to a professional singer I know, Stefan Youngblood, who recorded the song and performed it at his next concert. We played that song at the funeral also. I played it to my mom a week or two before she died, right after I got a copy of the song performed by Stefan Youngblood.

My mom and I both felt like it was a sign from God that she may be going home to Heaven soon, but had no idea how soon. I could see, being a physician myself, that she was going to die the night she did die, so I stayed up with her. I was prepared to stay up the whole night if that is what it took to be holding her hand when she died. I wanted to experience her glorious departure, having the wonderful experience of being with my dad the night he died a decade earlier and remembering the events of my maternal grandfather's death many decades earlier.

Because of her kidney failure, she went into a coma. I prayed that she would wake up before she died so I could say goodbye to her. And she did. She woke up as her breaths grew shallower and shallower. I told her the same corny joke I had told my father, believe it or not, about having to go to a special part of Heaven before they would let her in so she could learn how to dance. She was a fairly strict Baptist, so did not dance publicly. She actually laughed and said, "Don't worry, Paul, I already know how."

With her last breath, she squeezed my hand gently and whispered, "I love you, Paul." With that, her head dropped into my other hand and I had another parental death experience that I am sure will help prepare me for my own death someday. Whether I die suddenly, in my sleep, by myself or holding the hands of my wife and loved ones, I know I will not die lonely and "alone." I will die loving and being loved by the significant others in my life.

When we die someday, what good things could honestly be said about us? Will we leave a good legacy? King Solomon said, "The reputation of the wicked will rot (Proverbs 10: 7)." When death lies around the corner and you look back on your life, what do you want to see? Do you want to see the money you've earned or the people you've blessed? A client of mine this week had an awesome attitude about her own terminal cancer. Grieving? Sure she was, but she said to me very sincerely, "Death is part of life—a good transition."

> *"To the well-organized mind, death is but the next great adventure."*
>
> —J.K. Rowling

> *"In the valley of the shadow of death, remember, where there's a shadow there's a light! And it doesn't end there, we walk 'Through!' "*
>
> —Cynthia Spell

(CHAPTER FIVE)

My Super Bowl Dream

"Whether you see Him or not, God is at work in your life this very moment."

—**Chuck Swindoll**

The night before the 2013 Super Bowl, I fell asleep dreaming about swift running backs, aggressive middle linebackers, and long passes flying. But I woke up having one of what I have learned to call "my God dreams."

As a Duke-educated psychiatrist, I have been taught to place great value on dreams. I believe that every dream does have a meaning and is like a movie written by our unconscious, often revealing things we fear, or hope for, or celebrate for that matter. Most flying dreams for example are celebratory of succeeding in some phase of our lives. But being encouraged to think scientifically, we were taught to be skeptical and not dogmatic about the "interpretation"—our best guess—about each dream.

So to me personally, a "God dream" has been one in which God appears to instruct, warn or protect me, and I don't usually consider it a God dream unless some extreme coincidence happens the next day to reinforce that it wasn't just a simple dream about God. I have had dreams about the Father, the Son, or the Holy Spirit on various occasions, but on Super Bowl eve, Jesus was in this dream, reminding me of my "life verse" (favorite biblical passage) since I was 16 years old: Proverbs 3:5-6. In this passage King Solomon taught us, "Trust in the Lord with all your heart, and lean not on your own understanding. In all your ways acknowledge him, and he will direct your paths." Jesus told me to wake up and go look up the Hebrew word translated as "acknowledge" in that passage. So I did.

To my surprise the word implied to be aware of God's presence all around us, "behind the scenes" so to speak. He is often helping and protecting and blessing us in secret ways we are not even aware of. I decided to keep my eyes open for his presence more often, and to look at the "coincidences" in my life to see if they really were coincidences, or if some of them were loving nudges from God reminding me of his unceasing presence in my life. I was inspired by the concept and felt more loved by God.

Every human being on planet earth has the choice to see God in nothing, in some things, or even in everything. Some Calvinistic Presbyterians, for example, see God in everything and think nothing is a coincidence. I like to tease my Presbyterian friends by saying that if they fell down the stairs, they would get up, brush themselves off, and say, "Thank God that is over with!" Being personally skeptical, I don't really know what coincidences in my life are mere coincidences that occur in every life, and which ones may be God-directed for some unknown reason, or even if my Presbyterian friends may be correct. I have ruled out God being in nothing for reasons that will become obvious as we move along in this book.

The next day, after my God dream, I was looking for God's presence behind the scenes as my wife and I went to our neighborhood Super Bowl party, wearing my old blue jeans. I silently prayed for the safety of the players and selfishly hoped God would help my team win. Several players got injured, and my team lost!

It's a good thing God doesn't do everything I ask him to do. I am a warm and loving person, but admit to being narcissistic and spoiled enough already, and it would be detrimental to my character and to the rest of the world around me if he did say "yes" to me all the time rather than sometimes "yes," sometimes "no," and sometimes "wait."

After the game, my wife and I got home and changed into our pajamas to relax and watch some television. As I climbed out of my jeans a piece of metal surprisingly fell out of a pocket to the floor, having something inscribed on it in small print. My wife and I didn't remember ever seeing it before. It said, simply, "In all your ways acknowledge Him," and I have worn it ever since attached to my keychain. The Living Bible, in Acts 17:27, teaches us, "His purpose in all of this is that they should seek after God, and perhaps feel their way toward him and find him—though he is not far from any one of us." Acts 17:27 is a very interesting verse because in it God says he hopes we will reach out and seek him so we can see that he is already right beside us. I firmly believe that if our partially blind spiritual eyes were opened, we would be stunned by the extent of spiritual influences around us. From now on I will attempt to acknowledge God by reminding myself that he is right beside me, as he promised, even when I am not feeling his presence at the moment.

I am a scientific person so I realize fully that coincidences do occur. In fact, I am often quite a skeptic. But I have also taken many math courses including statistical analysis, and I calculated in my head the approximate chances that I would have a God dream about that one verse (Proverbs 3:6—"In all your ways acknowledge Him …") out of thousands of them in the Bible, then have a piece of metal fall out of my pocket the next day with that same verse inscribed on it. It was about one chance in a billion. God was reinforcing the fact that he is intimately involved in the details of my life. I felt very loved.

CHAPTER SIX

My Calling

O n a Sunday evening when I was 16 years old, an outstanding surgeon at our church came up to me and told me he and his wife would like me to come over to their home that night for coffee and donuts. He said they wanted to share some advice with me. I was so extremely in awe of him that I was honored to say yes and delightfully went. They told me they saw potential in me, and that, with very, very hard work, I could even become a doctor if I wanted. I was planning on becoming a carpenter like my father and maybe to start a father and son building business someday. I knew my dad would never take that risk without me pushing him, but he was a superb finish carpenter. But the idea of becoming a doctor did intrigue me somewhat, even though I wasn't planning on even going to college.

That surgeon was Dr. Bob Schindler, who later became a great missionary surgeon to Africa and later became president of the Christian Medical and

Dental Associations. But his advice to me was not at all to become a doctor. His advice was for me to memorize and meditate regularly on Proverbs 3:5-6, and to seek God's will for my career, not my own will apart from God. That is how that passage became my "life verses."

I promised Dr. and Mrs. Schindler that I would memorize those verses that very night, as soon as I got home. I promised to pray that I would end up in the career that God chose for me, whether that would be a carpenter, a doctor, a pastor, or whatever it might be. And when I got home I did pray, and I was very excited about it.

I had always been quite passive about my future career, thinking more about sports or who to date, not what to become. I was a "here and now" kind of guy, not a long-term planner. But now I discovered that a brilliant and godly doctor had faith in me, and that God was thinking about me and wanting to guide me into a career and a life calling of his choice for me. I became convinced that he knew what was best for me and had equipped me genetically and in psychological and spiritual ways to be the best at whatever he would call me to be or do.

That night I dedicated my life to God. I promised to use my future career and my entire life to help others improve the quality of their lives. I wanted my friends and others to become acquainted with the real God and to get to know him better as I was getting to know him. My father had read the Bible to our family every night at the supper table since way before I was even born. When I was six, my Sunday school teacher, Mrs. Brooks, helped me say a sincere prayer to let Jesus come into my heart to forgive me for the times I had done selfish things and to give me permission to live with him forever in Heaven someday. At age 10 I began reading my Bible on my own almost every night before going to sleep except for the nights I listened with a little earphone to the Detroit Tigers play baseball until the game was over. I hid my transistor radio under my pillow so my mom would think I was sleeping when she checked on me.

But I fell asleep that Sunday night at age 16, repeating over and over in my head King Solomon's advice in Proverbs 3:5-6: "Trust in the Lord with all your heart, and lean not on your own understanding. In all your ways acknowledge him, and he will direct your paths."

That night, in the middle of the night, Jesus was in my dream telling me, "Paul, I want you to become a doctor." I fell back asleep and had a second dream in which I was a middle-aged man and Jesus was telling me to go around the world teaching "practical Christianity." I was absolutely positive that God called me to become an MD, and to use that MD degree as a springboard to teach "practical, meaningful, and fulfilling lives" someday in foreign countries. It sounded impossible to me at the time. Little did I know that over the course of my lifetime I would not only go to college but get five degrees and write more than 90 published books that would sell eight million copies in more than 30 languages. Little did I know that I would travel all over the world training therapists, pastors, missionaries, and everyday people practical psychology and theology in a way that it would benefit them tremendously in their everyday lives. Little did I know at age 16 the dramatic extent to which those dreams would come true for this carpenter's kid, the son of German immigrants.

Teaching Practical Christianity Internationally

When finishing medical school, while trying to decide what field of medicine to specialize in, I was attracted naturally to psychiatry, the field where I could analyze and interact with and help people to understand themselves better and to find ways to live practical, meaning, and fulfilling lives. But back at age 16, I had two dreams that same night, and in the second dream Jesus told me I would someday travel around the world doing that specifically. But at age 47, that second dream had still not come true and I had pretty well forgotten about it.

I had already written dozens of books—about three a year from the time I finished my Duke University Psychiatry Residency at age 30. A few of those books had sold a million or more copies and were translated into various languages, so I guess I was fulfilling that dream indirectly but not by actually traveling to those countries and teaching "practical, meaningful, and fulfilling living." My books were all designed for that purpose, popularly known as "self-help" books.

But in my 40s I decided I would write a futuristic novel filled with adventure, romance, and political intrigue that would be based as much as possible on predictions in the Bible that, to the best of my knowledge, had never yet been fulfilled. So in my mid-40s, I memorized and meditated on Bible passages from every single chapter in the Bible that had anything to do with future or past predictions—known in theological circles as the field of Bible prophecy. In fact, I had taken courses on that in my 30s while obtaining one of my five degrees, a seminary degree from Dallas Theological Seminary. I studied under John Walvoord, the world's greatest Bible prophecy expert at the time. I admired him for being so objective. He was never dogmatic like some "Bible prophecy experts" about the meanings of the sometimes vague predictions. He would give each prophecy his best guess, but would often admit that we don't really know what many of them mean, but people in the future would understand them as their meaning became more obvious to them through circumstances in the world at that time.

My first novel was called *The Third Millennium*, and has so far sold about 700,000 copies. I finished writing it in 1992 and it came out in 1993. But in 1992, at age 47, I decided that I had to travel to Israel and Jordan to visit the places I was including in the novel, to be accurate. Some of the novel also took place in Newport Beach, California, where I had an office at the time and was familiar with the street names and other places I included in the book. But much of it took place in Israel and Jordan.

I still love the Indiana Jones series of movies, with Harrison Ford as the brave adventurer with a great heart for people. I especially loved *Indiana Jones and the Temple of Doom* (1984), which was filmed in Petra, Jordan, which should be one of the Seven Wonders of the World, it is so beautiful. It is an entire city where all the buildings and homes are carved into the soft rock of 700-foot-tall cliffs surrounding it. The only entrance into the city is between those cliffs in a path so narrow you have to ride into the city on horseback. The city has been largely abandoned for centuries. So I decided to have part of my novel take place there and actually traveled there, feeling a little like Indiana Jones myself. I believe the Bible predicts that masses of Jews will flee there in the future during a battle between Israel and the antichrist world leader and be supernaturally protected there. It is not far from Jerusalem, and the Old Testament uses its older name, Bozrah.

I traveled throughout Israel to see the specific places and street names and all that I wanted to include with great accuracy in my novel. While there, I decided to visit a large Messianic synagogue. There are many Messianic synagogues in Israel, throughout the United States (two just in Dallas where I currently live), and in other parts of the world. Worshippers there still have a rabbi, worship on Sabbaths, observe traditional Jewish festivals and some of the eating customs of kosher foods, etcetera, but they believe Jesus is the Messiah. They call him by the name he actually went by during his public ministry on earth, Yeshua. They believe Yeshua is coming back someday to rule the world from Jerusalem, along with the literal King David in David's new body he has in Heaven.

I don't speak Hebrew, so I snuck in late to the Sabbath service and sat in the back row where tourists were given earphones to hear a translator repeating the sermon in English. Nobody knew me there. I was a complete stranger to them. But the first thing I heard when I sat down was the rabbi saying, "There are about ten thousand of us in Israel who are believers in Yeshua (Jesus), and not a single professional Christian counselor among us to help those of us going through really tough times in our lives. So I want us to pray today that God will send someone, maybe even an American Christian psychologist or psychiatrist, to teach us as lay counselors things we can use to help our people in distress in types of problems not addressed in Scripture."

I had the chills and decided at that moment that I would come back and train them, finally fulfilling the second dream I had had as a 16-year-old to travel the world teaching practical, meaningful, and fulfilling lifestyles and healing the wounds that prevent people from experiencing that. I went up to the rabbi after the service and offered my services for free, even traveling at my own expense, and went there the next five years in a row to teach lay counselors from all over Israel, including Christian Palestinians.

The French Woman

To get home to Dallas, Texas, after that fateful trip to Jordan and Israel in 1992 at age 47, I had three flights: one from Tel Aviv to Paris, one from Paris to Chicago, and one from Chicago to Dallas. I was traveling alone, and, as you can probably guess, I like to talk to people and listen to people and analyze them and help them and learn from them myself.

On the flight from Tel Aviv to Paris, nobody spoke English on either side of me in the airplane, and I was bored to death. So on the twelve-hour flight from Paris to Dallas, I said a very earnest prayer to God: "Please, God, put somebody next to me who speaks English so I will have someone to interact with and won't go nuts from boredom." And to my pleasant surprise, a very attractive 30-year-old French woman from Paris sat beside me, and she spoke English fairly well. I prayed for God to keep my mind on her soul and not on her outward appearance.

Neither of us shared our names but we immediately struck up a pleasant conversation. I started by asking her where she was going, and to my surprise she was going to Little Rock, Arkansas, on vacation. I told her I had gone to medical school in Little Rock and that it was a very nice city, but asked her why someone from Paris would be going to Little Rock for vacation.

Her answer changed my life.

She told me that ten years earlier, she had been a college student in Paris, and that she had gotten very depressed when she and her fiancé had broken up. She said she got counseled by a missionary from Little Rock who gave her a copy of *Happiness Is a Choice* by Dr. Paul Meier, and asked me if I had ever heard of that book. I hid my shock and did not tell her that I was Paul Meier, simply saying, "Yes, I have heard of that book." She went on to explain to me that as a result of reading that book, she not only got over her depression but also became a believer, and was now a missionary herself in Paris, counseling college students. And she was going to Little Rock to visit her mentor who had given her the book and also "to hunt down Dr. Paul Meier."

Startled again, I asked her what she meant by hunting down Dr. Paul Meier. She replied, "The other missionaries in my group wanted me to get in touch with Dr. Paul Meier while in America. He has a chain of clinics and one of them is in Little Rock, so I am sure I will be able to get through to him by contacting that clinic and asking for his telephone number. They want me to ask him what advice he has for us to get more training in professional counseling here in France so we can help college students who have severe problems that are beyond the scope of biblical counseling, like bulimia or psychosis or other serious problems."

At that point I replied to her matter-of-factly, "Well, I am Paul Meier. When do you want me to come and personally train your group?" She thought I was teasing her and laughed until I pulled out my passport and showed it to her. She practically fainted. It was then that I totally remembered the second dream I had at age 16 about traveling the world someday to teach. A few days earlier I had promised a rabbi in Jerusalem that I would come and teach there. Now I was promising to come to Paris to teach there. My world travels had just begun. From that day forward for the next dozen years or so I traveled to about three countries a year to train people, including all over Europe, professionals from all over South America, and even Russia and Cuba.

A few months later, I was in Paris training dozens of missionaries, but also pastors and lay people wanting to learn what I was about to teach. One French man with three doctorate degrees, one in psychology, lectured some with me. His name was Dr. Jean-Luc Bertrand, and he is now my prayer partner. We email each other on an almost daily basis, even today.

CHAPTER SEVEN

My Experience with Henry Blackaby, Author of *Experiencing God*

I n 1990, Henry Blackaby was a guest on my daily live radio broadcast, "The Minirth-Meier Clinic," sharing with my listening family the awesome topics he covered in his book, *Experiencing God*. We had an average of two million listeners a day. I had just finished reading his book the night before, and sincerely prayed that night for God to give me a dream about Jesus—a dream I could share on the radio the next day with Henry as my guest.

And God did give me a dream. And I did share it, and will share that dream with you, but first ...

Henry was very genuine and a warm person, as I suspected he would be by reading his book and sensing his attitude throughout the book. One thing he shared with me and my listening family that day was, "If you really want to be in the will of God for your life, just look around you and notice all the things God is doing, and then find the one you really love and have a heart for and get on board." It was so simple while at the same time being alien to what most people think. Sure, I had a dramatic dream at 16 in which Jesus told me to be a doctor, and then a second dream telling me his will would someday include traveling around the world teaching practical living. But I still yearned to be in God's will in my day-to-day experience. I had lots of opportunities and invitations to do so many things, and I sometimes overcommitted myself and regretted it later. This made sense to me. Jesus said in Matthew 6:33 that his yoke would be easy, and his burden light, so when we feel like God is calling us to do too much and we are experiencing burnout, it is because we are probably confusing our demanding earthly fathers with our gracious Heavenly Father. I myself needed to heed Henry's advice and look over the opportunities set before me and pick and choose the few that would be most exciting to me and be part of my easy burden and light yoke from God.

While we were discussing Jesus, I told Henry on the radio what I had prayed for and then dreamed the night before. He was interested to hear the dream, so I told him and our listening family (and you, in my "reading family" right now). In my dream I was having a joyful walk through some pleasant woods, with birds singing all around me and the sun glistening through the leaves of the trees. I was far away from everything and everybody, just walking and meditating and enjoying my experience. Then all of a sudden, I heard a loud male voice just a few feet behind me shouting out, "Boo!"

I was totally startled and jumped into the air, turning quickly around to see who had snuck up on me out there in the middle of nowhere. And to my total surprise, it was Jesus, with his flowing dark hair and his white robe and sandals and all. And he was laughing loudly about how fun it was for him to scare me and sneak up on me, and I was laughing too by now, but at the same time pleasantly surprised by how cordial and calming and warm he was. He put his right arm around my shoulders and walked on with me on my journey through the woods carrying on a conversation about things I do not remember from the dream. Isaiah the Prophet taught us (Isaiah 30:21) that if you are a believer who is walking with God, "whether you turn to the right or to the left, your ears will hear a voice behind you, saying, 'This is the way: walk in it.' "

Henry and I discussed what the Bible says about God and how much he loves us and considers us his own sons and daughters. We discussed how he taught us in Psalm 139 that he was thinking about each one of us the night before individually, and that he thinks about each and every one of us each day so many times that we cannot even count them. And that he walks with us daily, with one arm leading us into his will, and the other arm hugging us and showing us his love. We are fearfully and wonderfully made in his image—his spiritual and emotional image, since God was without form until Jesus took on a human body. Jesus did so in order to live and suffer and die and resurrect to give us eternal life with him and to show us by taking on a human body that he wants to relate to us on a daily basis. He even misses us when we are out walking "alone" in the woods of life.

Jesus is equal in importance with God the Father and the Holy Spirit. When Jesus was baptized by John the Baptist, God the Father shouted out from Heaven in a clear voice, "This is My Son, in whom I am well pleased." Simultaneously, the Holy Spirit came down in the form of a dove so people would see him and landed on the shoulder of Jesus. All three of them interacted with each other at that moment in time. The three of them love each other, talk to each other, plan together, and have separate roles. They exist eternally as a spirit, or as three spirits united in some unfathomable way into one entity we call GOD. There is only one God but three unique spirits. Jesus did not always have a body that looked like our own. Philippians 2:6-11 teaches us that Jesus "thought it not robbery to be equal to God: but made himself of no reputation, and took upon him the form of a servant, and was made in the likeness of men. And being found in fashion as a man, he humbled himself and became obedient unto death, even the death of the cross. Wherefore God also hath highly exalted him, and given him a name which is above every name: that at the name of Jesus every knee should bow, of things in heaven, and things in earth, and things under the earth; and that every tongue should confess that Jesus Christ is Lord, to the glory of God the Father."

So how is this for a paradox? We were made in the likeness of God, but Jesus was made in the likeness of men (Philippians 2:7). We were made in the likeness of God emotionally and spiritually, and Jesus was made in the likeness of man physically. Meditate on how much he must really love us and want eternal fellowship with us.

(Chapter Eight)

My Dream about God the Father

S ince Jesus is the God-man, and Jesus sees his role to be to glorify God
the Father, what is God the Father like? The Father, Son, and Holy
Spirit are in total agreement and fellowship with each other but have
somewhat different roles and unique personalities of their own. According
to psychiatric research (as I explained in Chapter One), when we learn as
a young child to pray, "Dear Heavenly Father ..." we are often actually
thinking, "Dear Heavenly version of my earthly father."

Sigmund Freud noticed this in his patients and jumped to the
erroneous conclusion that God is only a father-projection and thus must
not exist at all. Freud was distant from his father and looked down on
his father and would unconsciously have a need, in my opinion, for a
Heavenly Father not to exist. His own father projections influenced his
way of interpreting the father projections he saw in his patients. We are
all prejudiced in our views of God by our own childhoods and other

experiences, even current rages over losses we have experienced and resent God for.

There are an almost infinite number of snowflakes, and yet no two are alike. There are seven billion people on planet earth, and if you had the time to ask each one to give you his or her image of what God is like, no two would be exactly alike either. But since there is a true God whom we can only partially comprehend in this life, all of us are partially wrong in our views of God. If my view of God were totally correct, surely there would be others who totally saw God as I see God in every respect, and nobody else on this planet does.

The purpose of this book is not to give you all the answers about who the real God is. In fact, my main purpose is to get you to ask so many questions and to become so unconfident of all your prejudices that you pray to him and seek him and trust that if anyone truly seeks to know God and to know his righteousness, he will be filled with God and experience God. None of us, before Heaven, will know all there is to know about God: only a fraction at best. The Apostle Paul implied that if he wrote a book filled with everything there is to know about God, and everything Jesus did, the earth could not contain it. It would be so large the earth would crumble.

Wanting to know more about God the Father, I prayed one night for a special dream about God the Father, and I had one. In the dream I was floating in outer space, all alone and scared absolutely to the point of death. I screamed out in terror, "I fear! I fear!" Then I was made aware of the omnipresence of God—God is everywhere at once throughout the universe and beyond the universe. God was everywhere around me that moment too and felt suddenly close by. Then I heard in a deep, loud, and clear voice, "I Am"… (a pause) "The Fear." And I understood what he was saying in his symbolic fashion.

God is the great "I Am"—he had no beginning and has no end. God is omnipresent (present everywhere in the universe at the same time). God is omniscient (He knows everything there is to be known, past, present and can even see every detail of what will happen in the future). God sometimes will begin answering our prayers before we even think of the request or ask him to. God started answering one of Daniel's prayers two weeks before Daniel asked it, because God can see the future. And God is omnipotent (He is all-powerful). In my dream, when God the Father told me, "I Am... The Fear," he was showing me that since he is the omnipotent one, if I have the type of fear of him that is reverential awe and trust, I don't need to worry about falling. The Apostle James said that we all fail in many ways. But when we do fall, God will lift us back up.

The Apostle Paul talked about his own failures in Romans 6 and 7, but concluded in Romans 8:1 that when believers fail, there is no condemnation. We just learn from our failures. Solomon said (Proverbs 24:16) that if a person fails seven times in a row but keeps trying, he is a righteous man. God holds us up to keep us from falling, but when we do, he lifts us back up without condemning us and says, "Well, what did you learn from that experience that will help you in your future?"

From my dream, I am now often reminded that, in spite of all my tremendous fear, I am surrounded by the great "I Am." I am surrounded by the eternal one.

We are finite human beings who see everything through our prejudiced eyes of having a beginning and an end, so people assume God must not exist because how could anyone not have a beginning? But they don't stop to realize that since we do exist, where did we come from, and when did the first matter erupt from the first energy, and where did the first energy come from to make the "big bang" or whatever the explanation may be? There had to be a supernatural power who always existed in order to bring energy and matter into existence. It is really narcissistic for us to think that just because we have never experienced eternal existence, it must not exist. As Einstein so wisely observed, studying the dependable laws of physics and the courses of the stars of the skies, a design implies a designer.

And God is "The Fear." After a pause, he also reminded me that he is The Fear. "I Am ... The Fear," he bellowed out to me like the low notes of a pipe organ in a huge cathedral. Believe it or not, The Fear is one of the names of God. It was The Fear who called Abram to become Abraham and find the Promised Land. The fear of God is said to be the beginning of wisdom, as wise King Solomon taught us. God was not saying to me that I should be afraid he would drop me. He wanted me to be aware that if I feared anything, it should be him and his power, not dropping out of the sky.

I felt totally at peace, secure, floating there in the presence of God the Father and bowing without even standing while in awe of him. The fear of God is reverential trust. I know God loves me, but I also know he disciplines his children out of love, and I also fear his discipline. I often pray, "Lord, teach me the easy way. Help me to obey rather than have to learn from my failures." I still often fail, but I think this prayer helps me fail less often.

(CHAPTER NINE)

My Dream about the Holy Spirit

|————————————————————————————|

Being so happy that God answered my first request to give me a dream about Jesus, and my second request to give me a dream about God the Father, I decided the next night to pray for a dream about the Holy Spirit, and what a big surprise that dream was.

In my dream that night, I was floating again, but this time it was not in outer space, and this time I was lying down in total peace and contentment in the arms of an invisible Holy Spirit. I could feel him cuddling me and holding me like a mother would a baby whom she loved deeply. And I was drinking milk more delicious than any I had ever tasted before—like warmed up milk mixed with honey—and I was drinking it from an enormous breast the size of my bedroom ceiling. I was the size of a baby, being snugly held and comforted and breast-fed, but I was a miniature version of my normal adult body. And then I heard the same deep voice I had heard in my Heavenly Father dream—so I assume it was his voice—telling me to wake up and get a Bible concordance and look up the name El Shaddai. And so I did.

When I looked up El Shaddai it is one of the names of God—Almighty God—not just the Holy Spirit but all of God. The concordance listed several implications for the meaning of the name El Shaddai, like "sustainer." I was startled to read that one of the meanings of El Shaddai was "God of the Breast"—the God who nurtures us.

Our human fathers and mothers loved us conditionally. Our Heavenly Father loves us unconditionally. Jesus loves us enough to become a human, suffer and die for us on a cross, even though we do not deserve it. And the Holy Spirit is our Comforter, who fills us with that unconditional love and enables us to feel that deep, unconditional love in the depths of our souls and spirits.

God the Father, the Son, and the Holy Spirit are eternal spirits united into one godhead somehow in a way impossible for us to totally comprehend. As an eternal godhead of three spirits, they were neither male nor female. They did not have sex organs until Jesus took on a human body and decided to become a man. In a sense, God the Holy Spirit is like the motherly aspects of God—the nurturing aspects of God. The Holy Spirit desires our love but does not ask for our attention. His role is to bring glory to Jesus and the Father.

The Holy Spirit pours God's love into us, even helping us to love ourselves in a healthy way so we have enough love in our own "love tanks" to in turn pour out our love to others. The Great Commandment includes loving God, loving others, and loving ourselves. The Holy Spirit empowers us to dance with the world, showing those around us the love of God. He chooses to love us. We don't earn his love. God gives it to us for free.

Ephesians 2:8-9 says, "For by grace (which means unmerited favor) are you saved, through faith, and that not of yourselves, it is the gift of God. Not of works, lest any man should boast." If we earned God's love, we would just get prideful and boast about it. Churches and denominations that teach us that we get to Heaven by being good are contradicting this and a host of other scriptures. We get to Heaven because God is good—by merely, as an act of faith, trusting God to forgive and save us and give us eternal life in Heaven because of what Jesus did when he paid for our sins on the cross. And the Bible says not a single human being would ever come to God without the loving call of the Holy Spirit drawing us to God through Christ's atonement, which means "at-one-ment." We become at one with God through salvation.

Ephesians chapter one tells us that the moment we trust Jesus to save us from our sins, we are sealed by the Holy Spirit until the day of redemption—the day we get to Heaven. We can't lose our salvation, because if we could, our salvation would depend on good works, and it depends only on the grace (unmerited favor) of God through faith in Jesus. We are sealed by the Holy Spirit until we get there.

If you owed a great financial debt and a rich man came up to you and offered to simply give you, as a gift, all the money you needed to pay all your debts from his immense wealth, your debt would still not be paid unless you had enough faith to accept the rich man's gift. If you accept the gift, you will be debt free. If you reject the gift, you will still have to pay for all you owe. If you ask the man what you have to do to earn the privilege of him paying off all your debts, he will tell you, "Absolutely nothing—just accept my gift. If you had to do something it would not be a gift at all—you would be earning it." The gift of God is eternal life. It is just one of his many gifts to us.

The Holy Spirit not only comforts us, draws us to Jesus, and seals us guaranteeing us salvation in Heaven someday, he also fills us. In the Old Testament days, the Holy Spirit would fill men and women of God for special occasions, like he filled Saul on special occasions even though Saul did lots of evil deeds in between those times. But after the resurrection of Jesus, on the Holy Jewish Festival of Pentecost, the Holy Spirit filled believers. And the Holy Spirit has been filling believers ever since.

Like Ephesians chapter one teaches us, every believer is filled with the Holy Spirit the moment we trust Jesus and we never lose that filling until the day we get to Heaven. But I think there are other "fillings" of the Spirit as well. There have been many times in my life when I have felt so close to God that I felt like I could almost walk up into the sky instead of walking on the earth. Don't worry, I never did! But the Bible encourages us in various places to be filled with the Spirit, so there has to be special fillings of the Spirit separate from being sealed until the day of redemption.

The purpose of this book is not to be a theology book or a book of facts as much as a book designed to help all of my reading family question their prejudices toward God taught to them erroneously by parents or churches or cults or demons. I also urge you to read *Experiencing God*, by Henry Blackaby, which is filled with beautiful passages of Scripture teaching us many things that draw us closer to God.

I pray that the Holy Spirit will use this book also, in a unique way, to draw its readers to God, but also to think more about who God really is, and to think about our misperceptions, and to realize his presence all around us, and to experience him with our emotional brain as well as our cerebral cortex. God gave us two brains, the cerebral cortex (the outer gray matter you see when you look at a picture of a brain) and a limbic brain.

The limbic brain is shaped like a hot dog, and it goes from front to back underneath the cerebral cortex, so you don't see it unless you turn the brain upside down. The limbic brain is the seat of our emotions. Jesus was in touch with both brains. Jesus wept. Jesus said those who weep are specially blessed, because they will be comforted (by the Holy Spirit). Jesus got angry at the moneychangers and others. Jesus was an emotional person and will eternally continue to be an emotional person and always has been an emotional God for eternity past.

Some people are so cerebral that they are not in touch with their feelings and make lots of horrible mistakes in their lives as a result of being out of touch. Other human beings are so emotional they don't take the time to think. You could throw away their cerebral cortex and you wouldn't notice much difference in their personalities!

Some Christians are so cerebral they are not in touch with the deep and loving emotions of the Holy Spirit. Some even make fun of those who are more emotionally in touch with the Spirit. I think they do this unconsciously so they won't recognize that they are missing out on some important aspects of their faith.

Other Christians are so emotional that they base their decisions and even their doctrines at times on feelings without using their brains to study Scripture enough to see if their emotional beliefs are contradicting facts God taught us in Scripture. Like the cerebral legalists, these overly emotional believers look their noses down on the cerebral group and think themselves spiritually superior to the cerebral group, just like the cerebral group sometimes think themselves superior to the emotional group. Satan loves to pit people against each other. There are humble and loving believers in both groups, but there are some arrogant and condescending narcissists in both groups too. God wants us to love one another. I consider myself a member of both groups in the brotherhood of Christ.

Proverbs chapter six lists the seven sins God hates the most. Sexual sins don't even make that top seven list, although they make the Ten Commandments. But the sin God hates the most is "a proud look," which involves thinking yourself more spiritual than or better than others, a sin we are probably all guilty of from time to time.

My goal is not to pit believers against each other, but to all humbly realize that none of us knows all the answers about God and none of us knows God perfectly. We are growing closer to him and will until the day we get to live with him in person forever in Heaven. So let's not condemn or look down on other believers for not thinking the way we do about God and our church doctrine. Let's love and respect each other realizing we are ignorant of a lot more things than what we do know. We are in search of a deeper knowledge of God—of him, not just about him! And the Holy Spirit desires that for us. If anyone seeks after true righteousness, the Bible tells us, he will be filled. May God fill us all with the Holy Spirit of God to draw us closer to Jesus and the Father, and to each other.

CHAPTER TEN

The "Real Us" and How We Find Ourselves

To get to know the real God intimately, it helps to get to know the "real us," and to mature the real us.

"Do you want to know who you are? Don't ask. Act! Action will delineate and define you."

—Thomas Jefferson

Three things determine who you really are—your genes, your environment, and your choices. This means your true self is the result of your genetic makeup and predispositions, lifelong influences from your environment, but most importantly, your personal choices. Whenever two people meet, there are actually six people present: the two as they see themselves, the two as they see each other, and the two as they really are. None of them is alike—so think about that awhile! Only

God knows the real "us." We ourselves don't even know the real us totally. All of us, as humans, are only guessing who "we" really are. If we learn to see others and ourselves more accurately, as God sees us, we'll grieve sometimes and rejoice other times, but the truth will help to set us free from the control of the unconscious over us.

The Defense Mechanisms

When people wanted to stone to death a woman caught in adultery, why weren't they trying to stone the man too? Chauvinism has been a sin throughout human history and remains a big one today. Jesus said to them, "Let him ... without sin ... throw a stone at her ... and they went away ... beginning with the older (John 8:3-9)." Older people tend to be more humble and willing to admit faults to themselves and to others. When I graduated from high school, I thought I knew practically everything. But the older I get, the more I realize how little I know. The more I learn about God, the more I realize how little I know about God too—outside the box. Are you mature, objective, and searching for truth? Then the wiser you become, the less certain and dogmatic you'll be, but you will love the real God more. A hand on a projector appears to be on the screen, but it is not. Likewise, our faults appear to be projected onto others. We see them in others (the "screen"), but not in ourselves (the "projector"). Matthew 7:3-5 describes this defense mechanism called "projection."

³ "Why do you look at the speck of sawdust in your brother's eye and pay no attention to the plank in your own eye? ⁴ How can you say to your brother, 'Let me take the speck out of your eye,' when all the time there is a plank in your own eye? ⁵ You hypocrite, first take the plank out of your own eye, and then you will see clearly to remove the speck from your brother's eye (NIV)."

In psychiatry residency at Duke, we studied "defense mechanisms," the 40 known ways that we lie to ourselves. Projection is just one of them. I described (with coauthors) the 40 defense mechanisms in our textbook, *Introduction to Psychology and Counseling* (Baker Book House, Publisher). Paranoid personalities use projection as their primary form of self-deceit, but we all use projection to some extent. Learning the truth about ourselves, others and God is the path to success.

Over the years, as a psychiatrist, I have found it easier to pray for patients than patience (patient endurance). Patience requires tribulation! But since my ultimate goal in life is to become more like Jesus, I honestly pray that God will send me whatever tribulations are necessary for me to grow—but to also help me to learn as much as possible and grow as much as is possible the easy way. If my true (rather than public) goal in life is to become more like Jesus in love and character, then I will appreciate tribulation to grow. So as I said, I often pray for more character and love, and sometimes for patience—but I pray, "Please help me, Lord, to be an easy learner (listening vs. suffering)."

Jeremiah 17:9 is a key verse to understanding Christian Psychology: "The heart is deceitful above all things ... who can know it?" God knows how little we understand ourselves and how much we deceive ourselves. I am sure God knows many more than just 40 ways we use defense mechanisms to deceive ourselves. One of my seminary students, years ago, found examples of all 40 in Scripture, plus more.

God knows us entirely and loves us and understands that we are mere fallen humans, saved by grace, and he has good plans for us. His plans? "For I know the plans I have for you ... plans to prosper you and not to harm you, plans to give you hope and a future (Jeremiah 29:11)." Solomon wisely advised, "Don't try to figure out everything on your own ... Don't assume that you know it all (Proverbs 3:5-7)." Pray for wisdom. Do you want a happy, valued life? Then love yourself, spill it to others, and "delight in the Lord, and He'll give you your heart's desires (Psalm 37:4)." If we see ourselves in God's eyes, forgiven and loved, we can love ourselves, delight in the Lord, and dance with all those around us to spread love!

T.D. Jakes teaches: *"Many of us are taking steps to discover our fallen brethren, but doing little to cover those they discover. Love covers a multitude of sins. The more we appropriately love ourselves in a biblical way, the less condemning we will be of others. And if we are mature, we will not be lazy about our journey.*

You may not walk on water; but you can move forward through a storm! You can't delay the journey just because you want sunshine!

Don't rush God's timing. Be confident that He has included you in His plan, even the details! Be still and sense God's purpose for your life.

Search your heart… somewhere there should be an inner knowing that directs you toward God's expected end for you. You have a purpose.

Remember to be honest with yourself. Denial is how we often get stuck in the muck and mire of life." —T.D. **Jakes**

Denial, by the way, is one of the 40 defense mechanisms. We meditate on Scripture, sin, confess, forgive ourselves, and analyze our sins to be set free from bondage—the truth sets us free (John 8:32). But we still will sin until we die, and John (in II John 2) says we are liars if we say we no longer do sin, so who are we to condemn others? And who are we to condemn ourselves either? God doesn't! (Romans 8:1). Not accepting God's grace and forgiveness for our sins is worse than the sins we originally committed. Jesus died and rose again so we could be forgiven. So today let's avoid as many sins as possible, confess, forgive, learn, and keep moving on to serve God and help others as much as we can. But when we have confessed, we need to get off our own backs too.

I want the "secret me" and the "real me" to become the same person.

Those who gossip and accuse us for our sins (true sins or often imagined ones or exaggerated ones) are sowing discord among the brethren. The Ten Commandments list ten of the 365 sins listed in Scripture, but Proverbs 6 lists "The Seven Sins God Hates the Most: 1. A proud look; 2. Sowing discord among the brethren … etcetera. Throughout human history, narcissistic people have "pontificated" and condemned, but now it even happens in public forums on the Internet.

A young woman came into my office crying, "Dr. Meier, I just can't figure out who I am!" I replied, "It doesn't really matter who you are!"

"Why doesn't it matter who I am?" she asked me. Then I replied to my client, "What really matters is who do you want to be? We have total freedom to grow into who we want to become, regardless of who you have been!" The Apostle Paul said (Philippians 4:13) that we can do all things if we ask God to help us.

Most humans think erroneously that they are trapped. Put grasshoppers in a jar with food and water supplies and holes in the lid so they can breathe, and they will try to jump out for about one day. After a day trying to jump out, grasshoppers give up and quit trying. Remove the lid and they won't ever leave even though they easily could. When we feel trapped we are just like those grasshoppers, deceived by others past and present, as well as by ourselves, into thinking we are trapped when we are not trapped. Free yourself today! The lid is off your jar.

I see clients daily in my Day Program, who come seven hours a day daily for three weeks and get six months to a year of therapy packed into those weeks. These clients change dramatically in that short three-week period! One client was the pastor of a 7,000-member church. He recovered totally from his depression, but wept in my office his last day as he was saying goodbye.

"Why are you weeping?" I asked him. His reply was, "As the pastor of thousands, I have seen many lives changed dramatically, but I've never seen people change so dramatically in such a short period of time as they have here!" When we learn the truth about ourselves by a therapeutic journey into our souls, share with others and God, and decide to change, we can and will.

Many therapists these days are actually taught to be passive and are a waste of time. We train our Meier Clinics therapists to dig for root problems. We don't tell our clients what to do, but rather what we see when we dig and probe their souls so they, with God's help, can free themselves. Getting to know the "real us" takes not only self-discovery by a variety of means but also self-determination, with God's help and guidance, to become who we want to become. King Solomon said if we store God's advice in our hearts, we will live many years, and our lives will be satisfying (Proverbs 3:1-2).

Unconscious Influences

Psychiatry research shows that about 85 percent of our basic personalities—our view of ourselves, others, life, etcetera, is determined by age six. Most people go through life not questioning all the lies they learned by age six about themselves and others, but thank God we all can change. Arrogant parents who are blind to their flaws see their own flaws in an exaggerated fashion within you (projection). Our lives can often be much healthier if we kick the negative messages of our parents out of our brains!

Some children grow up blind to their own flaws, rejecting innocent parents, imagining their own flaws in their parents—scapegoating them! As I said earlier, in my psychiatric training at Duke I studied 40 different ways that we lie to ourselves—defense mechanisms. Projection is just one of them. I love Paul Simon's song, "Something So Right," about how difficult it is for those who are used to being abused in childhood to accept love as adults, which is so right. In "Something So Right," Paul Simon sings about how the defense of the Great Wall of China is so much like the wall we have inside to avoid intimacy.

There's a wall in China 1,000 miles long, built strong to keep foreigners out. But there's a wall inside me that nobody can see, so it takes a long time to get next to me! At age two we were all emotional geniuses, crying when sad, laughing, hugging, and even sharing the truth—"I'm mad at you Daddy (or Mommy)." If our parents encouraged us to share our emotions, we stay emotional geniuses, but if punished for it, we fear emotions and repress them.

If sharing anger and sadness and other emotions is stifled in infancy, we feel falsely guilty for having them, with low self-esteem and shame. If we develop "toxic shame" from critical parents, we may become kind to others, but verbal terrorists to ourselves, unless insight changes us. Write a promise to yourself today, dating and saving it, promising to be your own best friend, kicking the critical parent out of your brain. Write it in the back of your Bible where you will see it and be reminded of your promise to yourself to become your own best friend. The written pledge should be to only say to yourself what you would tell your best friend under the same circumstances.

This significantly improves your quality of life. It will help you to see the positive truths about yourself instead of the negative false messages you received and erroneously believed in childhood. It will relieve much of your anxiety. Anxiety is a fear of finding out the truth about your own inner thoughts, emotions, and motives. In Psalm 139:23-24, David prays for God to reveal to him his own innermost anxious thoughts (unconscious thoughts) so David could grow from these insights and act maturely.

Overcoming a History of Abuse

People who grow up suffering from emotional, physical, sexual, and/or religious abuse tend to have low self-esteem. They feel foolish and are afraid to be assertive and to speak out.

> *"Better to remain silent and be thought a fool than to speak out and remove all doubt."*
>
> —**Abraham Lincoln**

Abraham Lincoln meant this as a joke, of course, but abuse victims actually think this way. Assertiveness is the confidence to let people know how you feel, to ask for what you need, and to resolve conflicts in constructive ways. Dr. Henry Cloud suggests, "Think of one person you are in conflict with and ask him this question: What have I not been hearing that I need to hear?"

If you don't see anything beautiful in the depths of your soul, get a "soul X-ray" because God sees a bunch of good character traits in you. He also sees your potential if you tap into your good traits.

> *"The worst thing you can die with is potential!"*
>
> —**Dr. Henry Cloud**

None of us will ever reach our full potential prior to Heaven. The world has still never seen what God could do with someone who is 100 percent dedicated to him and reaches his or her full potential. But we can all reach more of our potential than we have so far. Abuse victims also suffer from the horrible misperception that they somehow deserved the abuse. After enough abuse, they consider it inevitable and tend to repeat the abuse patterns in adulthood by picking abusive mates or friends or employers or even pastors. With proper therapy, abuse victims become as healthy as anyone else—often healthier. Their view of God may also change from seeing him as an abusive, mean-spirited God to a God of grace and love. They learn to see him outside the box of their own abuse-perspective.

King David promised (Psalm 9) that God is a stronghold for the oppressed, and (Psalm 68) that God will smash the heads of our abusers, in his timing. King David also promises in Psalm 68 that God will take us when lonely and abandoned and place us in a new "family." That is pretty awesome, right?

"Hope deferred makes the heart sick (Proverbs 13:12)." Waiting around for the approval of any abusive genetic family member is a big mistake. Love and be loved by the lovable who already love you unconditionally, as you already are.

One Form of Abuse is Religious Abuse

Some religions or individual churches try to make you feel guilty for existing, or for even loving yourself in a healthy way. They manipulate through guilt and toxic shame. There are 365 commandments listed in the Bible, but Jesus said if you only practice the Great Commandment (Mark 12:30-31) you will automatically obey all of the others. The Great Commandment is to love God, others, and yourself—you are God's precious child so why not love yourself biblically? You have to love yourself in a non-narcissistic, biblical sense to have enough love in your own love-tank to pour your love out on others. All sins hurt somebody. Even if there were no God, I would logically avoid sin as much as possible to enjoy life, and to love and be loved.

Three thousand years ago Jabez prayed (I Chron. 4:10) for God's hand to help him expand his wealth, but also to avoid sin so he would not cause pain. Contrary to some popular opinion—ironically by extreme political liberals and some legalistic Christians, wealth is not a sin, but a blessing.

Solomon advised us that if God blesses you with wealth, enjoy it but don't live for it. He wrote in Ecclesiastes 5:19, "Every man also to whom God hath given riches and wealth, and hath given him power to eat thereof, and to take his portion, and to rejoice in his labor; this is the gift of God." According to Mark 10:30, giving to God brings a 100-fold return. It may or may not be financially, but it will happen in one way or another. No other investment I have ever heard of guarantees to pay you back 100 times more than you invest.

When I graduated from Duke as a psychiatrist, I turned down two lucrative jobs to teach seminary students for $12,600 a year, but it was more than worth it! There was no "Christian Psychology" field yet, so I had to write my own textbooks, like *Happiness is a Choice*, *Love is a Choice*, and *Blue Genes*. Since then I have authored or coauthored more than 90 books, more than seven million copies in about 30 languages. God blessed me financially and in other ways. I later gave up my savings to keep my clinics nonprofit, but God has continued to bless me in many other ways. My wife and I live modestly, but God has blessed us. God has also blessed the national chain of nonprofit Meier Clinics, leading several million people to a relationship with God through its multiple ministries and spin-off ministries.

Abuse Leads to a Failure Script

What do you do with your "I can'ts?" When I was growing up, "can't" was considered the worst of all the "four-letter cuss words." I can do all things using Christ's strength (Philippians 4:13). We often fail because we are afraid to even try. Whenever you find yourself using the word "can't," change it to either "I will" or "I won't." Either alternative is fine. We don't have to try anything. But if there is something good that you would like to accomplish, say "I will" and pursue it until you either succeed or hit a brick wall that is beyond your control. You will at least feel good about yourself that you made the effort either way. If you don't want to try it, there is nothing wrong with saying, "I won't do that." Just don't ever say "I can't."

There are lots of good things that we could do but we simply don't have time to do and still keep our more important priorities. So there is nothing wrong with saying "no" to good requests from others if you don't have time or the desire to do that particular good thing. In fact, have the courage to say "I won't"—but don't lie to yourself or others by using that nasty "can't" word.

Many people have grown up or been subjected to such negativity that they develop a "failure script" whereby they feel "scripted" or predetermined to fail no matter what they do in life. They are often defeated before they begin.

Could Jesus think of many possible solutions to any seemingly "impossible" problem? Of course he could! He's God! So ask him to show you at least one of them. In Philippians 4:6-7, Paul says, "Be anxious for nothing"... ask God for solutions, even if we may not like one at the time, and God promises peace. Never ask God to carry out your specific solution. Are you smarter than him? Ask him to show you his best solution, even if it is difficult.

In King David's era 3,000 years ago, a lamp tied to your lower leg would guide you (Psalm 119:115). Meditating on God's Word is that lamp for you. I've been meditating on God's Word almost daily since deciding to at age 10. I haven't always heeded it, regretfully, but it always brings me back!

God promises to always be close to us, intimately involved every moment, so if he doesn't feel as close to you, who moved? He's not like your abusers. God wants us to love, be loved, and have an abundant life. But remember, "In this life we will have many trials and sorrows (John 16:33)." They are part of life.

I'm sure God protects us from many dangers, diseases, trials, and sorrows, but promises we will still have "many" (John 16:33), but helps us. Narcissistic Christians think they deserve no diseases, but I remind them that everyone Jesus ever healed died of something else later! And we all have struggles with difficult people from time to time in our lives. Someday we will soar with the eagles, but in this life we often have to deal with the turkeys!

As I've mentioned earlier, there are currently about seven billion people on planet earth and all of us to some extent or another feel like a nobody, and we go through life trying to prove that we aren't! The rat race means living to prove to others and ourselves that we are not a nobody—usually through sex, power, money, or prestige (fame). When a history of one form or another of abuse results in us having low self-esteem, we can either join the rat race, which always fails, or quit the rat race and live for God instead, resulting in a life of loving and being loved. King Solomon admitted (in Ecclesiastes) to personally trying sex, power, money, and fame, but found them all meaningless. Solomon himself went through a "Rat Race" time of his life. Only loving and serving God and others worked.

An Attitude of Grace

All of us are selfish at times. All of us have done things we regret. But Solomon calls people "righteous" who fail seven times in a row but keep trying. The Apostle Paul was a righteous man who admitted doing things he shouldn't and not doing things he should, but concluded in Romans 8:1, "there is no condemnation." The Apostle James said that we all fail in many ways, but grace replaces condemnation with "what can we learn from our ongoing failures?" The most evil people on this planet, according to Solomon (in Proverbs 6), are the arrogant religious legalists who condemn and look down on us.

In his public ministry, Jesus hung out with sinners often, but condemned the religious rule makers (scribes and Pharisees) more than anyone. For 40 years now, I have had a "prayer partner" and we confess our daily sins to each other without condemnation—grace. Confession heals us. The Apostle James (5:16) says that continued confession to other humans (to "one another") brings continued growth and healing. And the acceptance we get from those we have confessed to helps bring us into an attitude of grace toward ourselves.

An Attitude of Peace, Not Worry
Give God the Night Shift!

As a psychiatrist, many of my clients lie awake at night worrying, so I tell them to give God the night shift! In I Peter 5:7, the Apostle Paul also advises us to turn our worries over to Jesus. Perfectionists have what psychiatrists call "obedience-defiance" conflicts. Part of us wants to be perfectly good and obedient. But part of us wants to rebel and be disobedient. We will often be very good people but have small areas of our lives where sin sneaks in—holes in our consciences. Psychiatrists call these "superego lacunae."

When we worry during each day, we can't just turn it off in our own strength. Our obedience-defiance conflicts cause us to rebel against ourselves and worry even more. But there is a trick we can use to avoid worry, and it works very well. Instead, whenever you start to worry about something, promise yourself that you will worry about it on purpose that night. During each day, jot down your worries without worrying about them, then, at a special time that evening, pull out your list and pray about them. Keeping a "worry list" throughout the day enables us to put off worrying all day. It really works. Have a time each night to worry about them on purpose. When the time comes to worry about our "worry list" on purpose, we often realize how silly some are, pray about others, and then rely on God. It saves lots of time and hassle. Plus, when you try to worry on purpose, our brains rebel, and the worries tend to disappear.

Ninety percent of the things we worry about never come true. And the 10 percent that do, we grow from, so why worry? Great crises bring about great growth. When I ask older and wiser people what was their time of greatest spiritual growth, it is nearly always after their greatest tragedy.

We often worry about material things or other desires. The Apostle Paul taught us (Romans 8:32) that God loved each of us so much that he not only gave us Jesus, but also loves to give us all things. The Apostle Paul also promised each of us who believe in Jesus (Philippians 4:19) that God loves to give us everything we need—not want but need. The world can never bring us lasting peace—never has; never will! But Jesus promised eternal peace with a relationship with him—"Fear not (Isaiah 41:10)."

Years ago I was flying late at night from New York back to Dallas in a dark plane with my light on writing a book on anxiety. Lightning struck us. The lightning shook and lit up the plane as I was writing the Jesus quote to fear not! The pilot told us not to be afraid—that's what the lightning rods are for! That lightning striking the wing right outside my window while writing "fear not" brought God's peace into perspective. He is my lightning rod.

While writing about fear and anxiety, I decided to look up those words in my Bible concordance and found it discussed in every book of the Bible. From the longest books of the Bible to the shortest book (one chapter), the word fear (or anxiety) is mentioned at least once in every single book. God's gift is peace.

We fear potential dangers we are aware of. But we also fear things we are not aware of on a conscious level. Anxiety is a fear of finding out the truth about our own thoughts, feelings, and motives. When anxious, pray for insight into whatever it is you are afraid to see within yourself that moment. God urges us to do that in many passages.

The main purpose of Bible meditation (Hebrews 4:12) is as a "sharp sword" to reveal our innermost thoughts to us—our unconscious thoughts. In Psalm 139, King David says God thinks about you specifically all day every day, and then David prays for God to reveal to him his inner thoughts.

As a psychiatrist, my guess is that about 80 percent of our thoughts, feelings, and motives are unconscious, negatively influencing our lives. We gain insight into the truth about our innermost selves through Bible meditation, conviction of the Holy Spirit, and "a lot of counselors." God says that by using a multitude of counselors (including, I'm sure, both friends and professional pastors and therapists), there is safety. We pray (chatting with God off and on throughout each day), listen to constructive criticism from counselors, and meditate to discover truth.

The Holy Spirit sanctifies us by pushing up the truth from our unconscious to our conscious to deal with. We grow. We feel good about it. Our anxiety decreases for a time. And then the Holy Spirit "walks around" again in our unconscious and says to himself, "Hmm … what should Paul Meier work on next?" Then he pushes up another insight for me to work on. I feel anxious right before I finally let it up, then feel relieved again as I resolve it with God's help or the help of "counselors." And life goes on and sanctification goes on throughout my life. God never runs out of things to work on. If I live to be 100, there will still be unconscious areas of sin in my life for the Holy Spirit to push up or else I would be perfect, and nobody is perfect until we get to Heaven. God vows that this discovering and maturing process from the truths we discover about ourselves sets us more and more free.

Sanctification is the lifelong growth we experience from insights into the truth about ourselves. I continue to be shocked seeing more sinful thoughts or motives within myself the older I get. I grow from repentance (turning) from my sins, feel good about the growth, but then the Holy Spirit roams my soul to decide which sin to show me next! When reflecting over my entire life, I regret (but with no condemnation—Romans 8:1) my host of sins, but am thankful for God using me anyway.

God doesn't always take away our fears right away. Struggling with them awhile can bring growth. The Prophet Ezekiel (3:15-16) felt overwhelmed with stress one time, and seven days later God comforted him. Why did God wait? I don't know. But I'm sure there was a good reason. My ultimate goal and prayer is that God will help me, over the years, to become more like him, to serve him, to become better at resisting sin and to learn valuable lessons from the things I fear that do come true. So what is there to fear? Nothing but fear itself.

"Success is not final, failure is not fatal: it is the courage to continue that counts."

—**Winston Churchill**

(CHAPTER ELEVEN)

Predicting the Future

├──┤

"So we fix our eyes not on what is seen, but on what is unseen. For what is seen is temporary, but what is unseen is eternal."
—The Apostle Paul (II Corinthians 4:18)

We study the past and learn from the past, but set our eyes on the future, the "unseen," as citizens of an eternal kingdom. In Heaven, the Bible promises special rewards for those who read or hear the Book of Revelation (the main futuristic prophecy book) and for those who long for the return of Jesus to rule on earth. Instead of falling asleep tonight worrying about the events of tomorrow, try lying in bed tonight fantasizing what the future Messianic Kingdom will be like or what Heaven may be like. Fix your eyes on the future, but not exclusively of course. Some people are so Heavenly minded that they are no earthly good! But a balanced Christian life is where it's at. In Psalm 16:11, King David taught us, "Thou wilt show me the path of life: in thy presence is fullness of joy; at thy right hand there are pleasures for evermore."

Isaac Newton (January 4, 1643-March 31, 1727) was probably the most brilliant mathematician in history. But most people don't realize that he spent half of his time studying mathematics and half of his time studying Scripture—especially mathematical materials and predictions within the Bible. He even spent a great deal of time looking for "Bible codes"—where looking at skip sequences of letters in the ancient Torah might spell out other warnings from God. These have since been found to be true now that we have computers to find them.

I am a psychiatrist, but I also have spent a great deal of time meditating on and studying Scripture, almost daily since age 10. I memorized verses from every single chapter in the Bible that is in any prophetic book, having a particular interest, as did Newton, in prophetic numbers and predictions and fulfillments. I studied Newton's theological writings. By 1700 he had guessed that the return of Jesus to rule the earth would likely be sometime after the year 2000. And if he would have been alive in the 1940s, I suspect he would have booked a hotel room (or a tent) in Jerusalem on May 14, 1948, to be there on the day predicted for Israel to return to her land. Let me explain.

In Leviticus 26:18 and elsewhere, Moses gave a mathematical formula for the Israelites to remember. When Israel sinned greatly, God would give them a judgment and a specific time for that judgment, but would also give them a warning period giving them time to repent. If they repented, the rest of the judgment would be canceled. If they didn't repent by the end of the warning period, the remainder of the judgment would be multiplied by seven.

One such judgment was when God commanded Ezekiel (Ezekiel 4:3-6) to lie on his side in public for a portion of each of 430 days in a row, to teach Israel that God was judging them for their gross sins at that time (sacrificing babies, worshipping Molech, etcetera.) by expelling them from the land of Israel for 430 years. His contemporary, Jeremiah, said the first 70 years of Israel's exile would be in Babylon. That was Israel's warning period.

As predicted by Ezekiel and Jeremiah, sometime later, in 606 BC, Nebuchadnezzar came along and defeated Israel and transported most of them to Babylon (in and around modern-day Iraq). This began the 430 years of exile predicted by Ezekiel. And as Jeremiah predicted, exactly 70 years later, Cyrus the Great, King of Persia, defeated Babylon (536 BC). Amazingly, he offered to pay for the Jews to be transported from Babylon back to their native land of Israel (but still subject to him, of course). This was Israel's chance to repent and end the 430 years of exile. But by now the Jews had built their houses and businesses in Babylon, and the vast majority refused to go back to Israel. Only 50,000 took advantage of the generosity of Cyrus and moved back to their land.

Israel failed to repent by the end of their 70-year warning period, and this angered God, and so the mathematical formula of Moses now came into play: Ezekiel's 430 years of exile, minus Jeremiah's 70-year warning period in Babylon, leaves a remainder of 360 years of exile. According to the law Moses laid down in Leviticus 26:18 (and repeated elsewhere), the remaining 360 years had to be multiplied by seven, making it now 2,520 prophetic years that would pass before Israel is allowed to return to her land. For some reason, all the prophecies throughout Scripture were fulfilled in prophetic Jewish years of 360 days each.

So now simply multiply 360 days per prophetic year times 2,520 prophetic years left before being brought back to the land of Israel, and it comes out to 907,200 days. So take the exact day Cyrus made his decree to allow the Jews to go back at his expense, as recorded in history and in the Bible, and add 907,200 days, and it comes out precisely to May 14, 1948, the exact day that Israel became a nation again.

If you have had any courses in statistics, you will realize that the chances of this happening by mere coincidence would be less than one in a billion. So if your brain will allow you to look at facts that may contradict some of your prejudices against the Bible, you will have to admit that the chances of the Bible being true and the God of the Bible existing and being the real God, just based on this one prophecy alone, are a billion to one. And every prophecy in the Bible predicted to happen in the past has been fulfilled also in as precise a manner. Claiming to be a prophet and making any prediction whatsoever that did not come precisely true was punishable by death. They were not like modern-day fortunetellers who get lucky once in a while. There is not a single prophecy in the Old Testament that was supposed to happen in the past, not the future, that has not come precisely true after it was predicted and recorded.

Liberals in past decades assumed that Ezekiel and Daniel and Jeremiah and the other prophetic books must have been written just before Christ was born, pretending to be older books and predicting most of these things after the fact. But with the discovery of the Dead Sea Scrolls, these same books were intact and stored in clay jars 2,000 years earlier by the Essenes in Israel and radiocarbon dated to 700 years before Christ, during the exact times in history they claimed to be written in.

I could fill an entire book with the Bible's predictions of future events that were precisely fulfilled, but that is not the intent of this book. One short chapter will suffice. So let me share just a few more mathematical things that I hope are as inspiring and exciting to you as they are to me. Then I will make some of my own purely theoretical guesses about the future based on my own interpretation of prophetic passages, some of which are purposely vague. God obviously wanted some future predictions to be clear, and some to be vague until future events will make these passages more clearly come alive.

The reason prophecies are so exciting to me is because when I was 22 years old, I was an "Alumni Distinguished Graduate Fellow" on scholarship at Michigan State University grad school in cardiovascular physiology, and I thought I was pretty smart. I was quite prideful and still cannot brag about any great degree of humility! I had used the scientific method to almost reason myself into giving up on there being a God or if there was, having him not be the God of the Bible. I studied the other religions and found them wanting as well.

Psychiatrist Paul Tournier says it is good to have a time of doubt like this, so you can take off the religious overcoat of your parents, then take a good look at it, and if it is correct, put it back on with some modifications if necessary. But now it is your own coat and no longer the coat of your parents. Fortunately, I studied Bible prophecy and the statistical analysis of these things coming true by coincidence rather than by divine intervention, and came to the overwhelming conclusion that the Bible and Christianity (not any particular denomination) were true beyond any reasonable doubt. And that was that.

The Old Testament predicted that the Messiah would come twice, once as a lamb and once as a mighty roaring lion. A "former rain" of blessings on Israel and a "latter rain"—and according to Hosea 6 there would be "two days" in between them. In the Bible, a day with the Lord is like 1,000 years on earth, so that could mean approximately 2,000 years between the death and resurrection of Jesus and the Second Coming of Jesus. Isaac Newton thought so. Irenaeus and Hippolytus, second century theologians who were students of the writings of the Apostle Paul, also thought so.

The Old Testament predicted that when the Messiah came the first time, as a lamb, he would be born in Bethlehem (Micah 5:2), a city known for the raising of lambs. It predicted that the Messiah would be betrayed for 30 pieces of silver (Zechariah 11:12). Zechariah, written about 700 years before Christ, also predicted future wars in which there would be such instantaneous intensive heat that the skin of people and horses would melt completely off before the skeletons had time to fall to the ground, which could only be a description of nuclear warfare reasonably (in Zechariah 14:12). Zechariah (9:9) also predicted the Messiah would ride into Jerusalem on the humble foal of a donkey, which Jesus did.

In Daniel 9:24-27, Daniel predicted that someday in the future there would be a decree made to rebuild the walls of Jerusalem. When that decree would be made, then exactly 69 "weeks" of years later (69 X 7 = 483 years), the Messiah would make his official entry into Jerusalem. Four hundred eighty-three prophetic years times 360 days per prophetic year, comes out to 173,880 days. Now please stay with me and don't get lost with all these numbers. The only decree ever made to rebuild the walls of Jerusalem was made by Artaxerxes Longimanus, recorded historically as happening on May 14, 445 BC and also recorded in Nehemiah 2:1. So now take that date and add 173,880 days and it comes out to April 6, 32 AD, the exact day that Jesus made his triumphal entry into Jerusalem on the foal of a donkey. A good mathematician could have booked a hotel room to watch that event years in advance! The Old Testament also predicted that on his first coming, the Messiah would be "cut off"—which certainly happened at the crucifixion.

When the Messiah (Jesus) comes a second time, his "latter rain," (comparing it to the rains in late summer that prepare the second crops), it will be to fight the Battle of Armageddon, defeat the antichrist and his world government, and rule on earth as the Lion King for 1,000 years before creating a new earth. The new earth will be even more wonderful than ours is at its best.

"In the new earth nothing good is lost. The music of every pleasure is transposed into a higher key."

—John Piper

The Bible says nobody can predict accurately when the Messiah will return for his second coming to earth to reign here. The Bible is purposely somewhat vague, but with lots of hints.

Jesus said in Matthew 24 that before he comes back to rule on earth, there would be more and more earthquakes—major earthquakes—like a woman in birth pains. And there have been a vast increase in the number of major earthquakes during each of the past ten decades. He also said there would be an increase in ethnic groups rising up to fight other ethnic groups. The English translations say nation against nation but the original Greek implies ethnic groups against other ethnic groups. With the terrorism in the world today, we have certainly experienced that as being on the rise.

There will also be "signs in the heavens"—and we don't yet know what they will be. I believe one such event was the comet Shoemaker-Levy 9. Wikipedia states, "Comet Shoemaker–Levy 9 (formally designated D/1993 F2) was a comet that broke apart and collided with Jupiter in July 1994, providing the first direct observation of an extraterrestrial collision of solar system objects."

When the comet was first discovered, scientists did not know the exact day it would hit or how many parts of the comet there would be or how long it would take for them to hit or what the extent of the impact would be. Since in the end times there will be a New Roman Empire with the antichrist as its leader, and since Jupiter is a god of the Romans, I made a few guesses of my own and told my family and friends that it was a mere speculation, which it was. I guessed that it would hit on the 9th of Av (an annual day of mourning for Israel), and that since the tribulation period will be seven years long and have 21 judgments, the comet Shoemaker-Levy 9 might possibly have 21 large separate parts that hit Jupiter over a seven-day period. I was more shocked than my family and friends when, a few weeks later, scientists said the date it would hit (which was the 9th of Av in Israel), and that it would have 21 large rocks that would take seven days to hit Jupiter, and that the impact would be significant. But I am not a prophet at all, and I may have just gotten very lucky, so please do not misunderstand me. It was just very interesting and aroused curiosity in me.

The New Testament, in II Thessalonians 2, vaguely hints that nobody will know who the antichrist is until after believers are raptured off this planet, when the Holy Spirit's restraint is removed, prior to the second coming of the Messiah. But Daniel predicted 700 years before Christ (in Daniel 9:24-27) that the antichrist will sign a seven-year decree promising to protect Israel and that will start a seven-year countdown until the second coming of the Messiah, so probably seven times 360 days after the decree is signed. But national leaders have signed many peace treaties with Israel so we won't know which decree is this one until other events make it obvious. The antichrist will double-cross Israel and declare himself to be their god three and a half years after signing the decree, and he will immediately become like Hitler and kill millions of Jews worldwide. Revelation 12 says the Jews who get killed will be Jews who have come to believe that Jesus is their promised Messiah.

Before ending this chapter, please allow me to share with you some historical facts that may very well astound you. If you are a student of the seven feasts of Israel, which I have always been fascinated by, you will know that there are two annual "fast days"—days to mourn and fast for Israel's past two greatest days of lack of faith. Moses broke the Ten Commandments on the 17th day of the month of Tammuz, so Moses made that a perpetual fast day in Israel to this day. And when Moses sent 12 spies into Palestine to spy out the land to see if Israel, with God's help, could defeat them, 10 came back saying there is no way Israel could win. The Jews were like grasshoppers compared to the large men who lived in those nations, they said. This lack of faith made God very angry, and that occurred on the 9th day of the Jewish month of Av, so every year devout Jews fast and pray on the 9th of Av to this very day. The Old Testament predicts that someday in the future these two fast days will become feast days of celebration (I think during the 1,000-year reign of Jesus).

Having said all this, here is what may astound you: In 587 BC, the Babylonians broke through the walls of Jerusalem after a two-year siege and stopped sacrifices for the first time in more than 400 years, and they did this on a 17th of Tammuz. Twenty-one days later, on the 9th of Av, they destroyed Solomon's temple.

In 70 AD, Titus and the Roman legions besieged Jerusalem and catapulted enormous stones against the walls of the rebuilt temple, killing many priests and stopping sacrifices. According to the famous Jewish historian Josephus, this occurred on a 17th of Tammuz. You guessed it. Twenty-one days later, on the 9th of Av, the temple was completely destroyed and burned down to melt the gold between the stones, and not one stone was left upon another, as also predicted in the Bible before it occurred. Micah 3:12 predicted 700 years before Christ that Jerusalem would someday be plowed into a secular city, which occurred in 71 AD on the 9th of Av.

In 135 AD, Simon bar Kochba led a Jewish uprising against Rome. His army was totally wiped out by the Roman army on the 9th of Av of that year. The Crusades began when Jews were killed on the 9th of Av in 1096 AD. The Jews were expelled from England on a 9th of Av in 1290 AD, and expelled from France in 1306—you guessed it again—on the 9th of Av. The final day for all Jews to leave Spain (unless they converted to Catholicism) was August 2, 1492, which was again, a 9th of Av. It also happened to be the same day

Columbus sailed the ocean blue to discover America, a place where Jews would be protected for more than 500 years now.

I personally believe that Columbus was secretly a Jew himself, a Jewish Italian from an area where many Jews lived. July 4, 1776, the day America became a nation, was a 17th of Tammuz, the reason for which I do not understand but have my suspicions that America may reach a point, and is close already, where it no longer is the main protector of the nation of Israel and of the Jewish people. The main protectors of Israel in America are evangelical Christians. Paradoxically, the vast majority of Jews in America vote for national political leaders who consistently vote anti-Israel and pro-Palestinian. I gathered this information over dinner directly from a well-known Jewish writer for both the *Jerusalem Post* and *The New York Times*.

Polish Jews were massacred in 1648 on the 9th of Av. The pogroms against Russian Jews (as shown in the great movie *Fiddler On the Roof*) began in 1882 on a 9th of Av. When World War I began, Jews were immediately persecuted in Russia. The war began on the 9th of Av, 1914. And on the 9th of Av, 1942, that was the very day that Hitler and his henchmen had their official meeting in Wannsee, Germany, to come up with their final plans for the killing of all Jews worldwide. If all these "coincidences" don't convince you that the God of the Bible is the only true and real God, what will?

Using the ancient names for these current countries, Ezekiel predicted in Ezekiel 38-39, nearly 2,700 years ago, that there would be a future war between Russia and Israel, with Russia's allies to include Syria and other Arab nations nearby. But God will deliver Israel, wiping out five-sixths of the Russian army with "fire and brimstone"—nuclear bombs from Israel? There is also a "country from the East" that has 200 million soldiers that will cause a world war, destroying a third of mankind before being defeated. China has announced publicly that it has 200 million soldiers. This prophecy was made when the entire population of the world was only a few million. It must have seemed ridiculous at the time. If the Muslim nations ever could unite instead of killing each other, they could also come up with 200 million soldiers. There are more than a billion Muslims who control about a quarter of the area of earth. Israel is a tiny nation, and only has about five million Jews. Get that in perspective.

Do you still have any doubts about the God of the Bible being the only true Creator-God? I would feel like a very foolish person not to believe with all the obvious mathematical evidence alone. And what I have shared in this short chapter only scratches the surface of all the other prophecies throughout Scripture that have been precisely fulfilled.

"We are to use our intelligence, which is usually an instrument of independence, to make us increasingly dependent on God."

—John Piper

What about the Near Future?

In spite of being a psychiatrist, I wrote four Bible prophecy novels, so I am often asked what the Bible says about the coming antichrist. Prophetic passages about the future are often purposely vague and open to various interpretations, so I can only make the best guesses I can base on my own interpretations of these passages. But I would like to make some guesses at this time.

The Bible never says Israel will consider antichrist as their messiah. He will make a seven-year peace treaty to "protect" them but not keep it.

Antichrist will be a Gentile (from the "sea" of Gentiles), but his religious leader (false prophet) will be from "the land" = Jewish descent. Antichrist will be from a relatively young nation ("little horn" means young, not small) that descends from the old Roman Empire, likely the United States of America, since it is a relatively young nation that descended from the old Roman Empire, and it is the most powerful nation on earth still at the time of writing this book.

Antichrist will be so powerful militarily that he threatens his way to the top of the new Roman Empire (a bow with no arrows). Isaiah mentions "tall, fair-skinned people from the west," and the Bible mentions deliverance initially "on eagle's wings"—U.S. airplanes? So it is not fair for prophecy "experts" to assume there is no mention of the United States in future prophecy. I think there is a great deal, depending on how one interprets certain passages.

Antichrist will be a wolf in sheep's clothing—a hero to most but extremely evil behind the scenes, making bad good, and good called bad. Antichrist will "have no regard for women" in spite of acting like their defender—either chauvinistically or religiously or sexually. Antichrist will shock the world by surviving a "head wound"—either literally or figuratively by regaining power after political death.

Antichrist most likely will be a future American president, riding a "white horse" as a hero to leadership of the future United Nations. I think the future antichrist will be a future US president, most likely, because he will be from the most powerful nation militarily that also is a relatively young nation descending from the ancient Roman Empire, which the USA is.

Some of antichrist's genetic relatives will descend from Titus of the Roman army that destroyed Jerusalem in 70 AD. So he has to be a Gentile. Plus the Bible says he will come from the "sea"—which I do not think means from the literal sea or ocean, but refers to the sea of Gentiles, a common figure of speech in Old Testament times. Nobody will know for sure who the antichrist is until after "the Holy Spirit is removed" temporarily from the earth (the rapture), based only on vague hints from II Thessalonians chapter two. So go ahead and guess all you want whether this person or that person could arise to become the antichrist. You probably won't ever know for sure until after the rapture, which is described in I Thessalonians 4. So you will be in Heaven when you find out, if I am guessing correctly, unless you are a nonbeliever and figure it out after all the believers in the world disappear suddenly, and the world believes a lie about why and how it happened.

Antichrist will eventually rule the United Nations from the "city that sits on seven hills"—the Seven Hills of Rome. Antichrist will have heavy taxation, taking money from the wealthy and redistributing it in unfair ways to his own friends. We don't know what his religious affiliation will be at first, but will emerge as the world's messiah, and eventually impose emperor worship of himself. Halfway through his seven-year peace treaty to protect Israel, he will go to the temple area, desecrating it like Antiochus IV

Epiphanes did in 168 BC. He will immediately begin killing Jews as they flee from Jerusalem and the rest of Israel.

Millions of Jews worldwide will be killed in a holocaust worse than Hitler's, and Revelation 12 indicates that most of those Jews who will be killed will be Jews who believe in Jesus as their Messiah. Apparently, after the rapture, millions of Jews will realize that Jesus was truly their Messiah all along, while most of the rest of the world will believe a lie about the rapture.

The rest of the world will likely think the Christians were taken out of the world because of their bad karma or some other negative reason. Alien abduction is another possible false scenario to blame. Most will not believe the truth—that it is Jesus rapturing out believers and their children (hopefully all children), leaving the rest behind to suffer the seven-year tribulation period or whichever portion of it remains at the time of the rapture.

The Bible nowhere dogmatically or clearly says that the rapture will happen prior to the seven-year tribulation period. It could happen quite a while before the seven-year tribulation begins, right before (most likely, but I can't be dogmatic), during the tribulation, mid-tribulation, or even near the end of the tribulation. Dr. John Walvoord, former president of Dallas Theological Seminary, was the world's leading authority on Bible prophecy at the time that he told me God purposely made many end time events vague, so it would be unclear to us now, but become clear to the millions who become believers during the tribulation and are then suffering through the 21 judgments listed chronologically in the Book of Revelation.

Even though Walvoord believed the pretribulation rapture to be most likely for a variety of reasons, I still remember when Russia invaded Afghanistan and Dr. Walvoord walked into our faculty lounge and said to us, "I sure hope we are right about the pretribulation rapture!" He thought that war could be a sign of the tribulation. He taught me that he felt the pretribulation rapture was merely a good guess, and that we could not be dogmatic about it.

As I said, Revelation 12 says the antichrist will kill two thirds of the Jews, but the ones he kills are Jews who follow Jesus (after the rapture). There are probably only about 20-30 million Jews in the world today, so if there are 30 million, 20 million will be killed by the antichrist in the final holocaust.

When antichrist declares war on Jewish Christians (Revelation 12, etcetera), many will flee from Israel to an area God protects them in—Petra (Bozrah). Petra is a walled city, relatively uninhibited, in Jordan, 70 miles from Jerusalem. Jesus will go there first to gather his "lambs" after the Battle of Armageddon has been won. A revived "Babylon" will be sitting on the Euphrates River (Iraq and the other Arab and Persian nations re-united—led by the Muslim Brotherhood?). There are two "Babylons"—religious, materialistic "Babylon" and literal Babylon on the Euphrates River (united oil nations), and the latter will "sit on" (gouge) antichrist for money—apparently money for oil. There are two main denominations of Islam, the Shia and the Sunni Muslims. They are frequently at war with each other, and Iraq is divided religiously into those two factions, with Iran being Shia but Turkey and Saudi Arabia being Sunni. Watching the news programs about these major differences makes it difficult to believe they will someday unite into a New Babylon. The ancient city of Babylon was rebuilt in Iraq by Saddam Hussein prior to his defeat by the United States. Just keep watching the news about the Middle East, and you will be watching Bible prophecy being fulfilled in stages only God knows.

Antichrist will initially be a close ally of the United Revived Babylon, maybe even like a messiah to them, but will resent them for financially gouging him. Toward the end of the seven-year tribulation period, antichrist will turn on them. Antichrist will double-cross his Babylonian allies before the Battle of Armageddon by blowing the city of Babylon (nuclear probably) into the Persian Gulf.

Antichrist will also defeat a "people from the east with 200 million soldiers" (China has that many now counting reserves, but it could be Babylon, with more than a billion Muslims in the world today). But before the "country from the East with 200 million soldiers" is defeated, they will manage to kill about a third of the world population through war, resulting famine, diseases, and wild animals. These are almost certainly the aftereffects of nuclear war.

Believers throughout history, including raptured believers, will return with Jesus for the Battle of Armageddon with all his angels and win. Jesus will throw antichrist alive into Hell, then go straight to Petra to gather his "lambs" (Jews) protected there. The Bible says Jesus will lead that group, followed by all the rest of us, into Jerusalem, through the Eastern Wall (kept closed by Arabs now).

Matthew 24 and Daniel 12 say the "end times" will be marked by a rapid explosion of knowledge (obviously referring to the computer age), more and larger earthquakes, ethnic uprisings, and cosmic signs. Russia will unite with nations around Israel against Israel but will lose, with the vast majority of their armies killed by earthquakes and fire from sky. God will supernaturally protect Israel, even if it includes using nuclear weapons Israel already has in place, possibly even in places hidden in other nations surrounding them. The earthquakes and "fire and brimstone" could be caused directly by God, or indirectly by nukes Israel may already have buried. The Prophet Zechariah, in Zechariah 14:12, I am quite certain, was describing nuclear warfare 700 years BC. The Bible is not clear when this particular Russian battle will occur, and it could occur at any time, even during the year you are reading this book.

So that ends my summary of some of my best guesses of what could occur in possibly even in our own lifetimes, but remember that God's Word often stays purposefully vague about future prophesies that have not yet come.

CHAPTER TWELVE

Experiencing God Outside the Box through the Eyes of C.S. Lewis

---

"Pain is God's megaphone to rouse a deaf world."

—C.S. Lewis

We are all growing older, and as we do, we come to realize that the times in our lives when we experienced the greatest growth spurts emotionally and spiritually were nearly always right after our most painful experiences. Sometimes I lift weights, but the rule of thumb for lifting weights is "no pain, no gain." I have to lift enough weight for enough repetitions so that there is pain in the muscles I am trying to build, or else those muscles will not grow stronger. The same is true of life, so I began this chapter with that C.S. Lewis quote.

An Analysis Of C.S. Lewis:

C.S. (nicknamed "Jack") Lewis was born Clive Staples Lewis in Belfast, Ireland, November 29, 1898. He died in Oxford, England, a week before his 65th birthday, on November 22, 1963, the same day that President John F. Kennedy was assassinated. He was an outstanding scholar, a professor at both Oxford (1925-54) and Cambridge (1954-63) universities, an author, radio broadcaster, and possibly the greatest Christian apologist of the century. A Christian apologist is someone who has a compassionate desire to help people understand Christianity, and to share the conclusions he has come to about Christianity, so he writes about and speaks about the many reasons why he believes Christianity to be true.

His books sold millions of copies in more than 30 languages. He was a former devout atheist who was gradually convinced of the truths of Christianity by his good friend and fellow author and scholar, J.R.R. Tolkien, and some other close friends. Tolkien was an evangelical Roman Catholic and the author of *The Hobbit* and *The Lord of the Rings*. Lewis wrote numerous books, including *The Chronicles of Narnia*, *Mere Christianity*, and *The Screwtape Letters*.

C.S. "Jack" Lewis became a member of The Church of England, but considered himself a Christian first and foremost and not a defender of any denomination. In *Mere Christianity*, he defended the basic core beliefs that the various denominations of Christianity share in common.

As a psychiatrist, I have two goals for writing this chapter for you, my reading family. My first goal is to analyze the life of C.S. Lewis to understand his most likely unconscious presuppositions that led him to become an atheist. Then, upon becoming persuaded to reluctantly become a "theist" at age 30, it took him nearly two more years of studies, experiences, and sharing with his Christian friends to finally put his faith in Jesus as his Lord. He was 32 years old at the time.

My second goal is to share with you the deep-rooted beliefs of C.S. Lewis as his studies and his experiences with God and with others led him away from his childhood presuppositions to an experience of God that was definitely "outside the box." I hope you, my reading family, come to understand what it is like to experience God outside the box through the eyes of C.S. Lewis.

C.S. spent his early years in Belfast, Ireland, a part of Northern Ireland made up predominantly of Protestants loyal to England, many of whom were originally of Scottish descent. His father was an odd, eccentric, and distant lawyer. Growing up distant from his father led C.S. to be especially close to his dog, Jacksie, who was struck by a car and died when C.S. was four years old. C.S. was at such a loss when his dog died that he wouldn't even talk to people for a while after that unless they called him Jacksie, which became his nickname, becoming shortened to Jack as he got older. That remained his nickname throughout his life.

An even more painful loss was at the age of 10, with the death of his mother, Flora, the daughter of a Church of Ireland (Anglican) priest. She died of cancer. C.S. was the second of two sons. After the death of his mother, C.S. was shipped off by his eccentric father to various boarding schools. As a psychiatrist, I would assume he felt bitter and abandoned by his father, and I believe this is what led him to project his father image onto God the Father and abandon his Christian faith in his early teens. He was a brilliant student and won a full scholarship at age 18 to University College, Oxford. But before he could start college, he was drafted to fight in World War I.

In the army, he became close friends with his roommate and fellow cadet, Paddy Moore. They made a pact with each other that if either of them died in the war, the survivor would take care of both families. Paddy was killed in the war in 1918, so C.S. kept his word and became close to Paddy's mother, Jane King Moore. In fact, they spend so much time together that C.S. would introduce her as his own mother. He took care of her until she died of Alzheimer's disease in 1951, visiting her almost daily in the nursing home for years. During the war, C.S. was also wounded and spent some time in a hospital recovering. Jane Moore, his "adopted" mother, came to visit him daily, in contrast to C.S.'s eccentric, demanding father, who never came to visit him a single time.

After the war, C.S. completed his academic training and became a professor at Oxford University in 1925, at the age of only 26. C.S. and fellow faculty member J.R.R. Tolkien became close friends, and both became active in an informal Oxford literary group that called themselves "The Inklings." It was after a long evening walk with Tolkien one night, when C.S. was 32 years old, that C.S. became a true believer. Lewis grew deeply in his faith over the years, and even defended Christianity on regular radio broadcasts during World War II in England, which brought him wide acclaim. C.S. remained single most of his life, but in his late 50s he began corresponding with an intellectual American writer named Joy Davidman, who was 17 years younger than C.S. She was of Jewish descent and had at one time been a communist and an atheist, but became a devout Christian.

She was in the divorce process when they began corresponding as friends, purely for intellectual reasons initially. Later they met and fell in love and were married in 1956. They grew to love each other deeply, and in the most painful time of C.S.'s life, he watched her die of cancer only four years after they got married. She was 45 years old and he was 62. C.S. had lost his beloved dog at age four, his mother at age 10, his best friend Paddy at age 20, Paddy's mother who had become his own "adopted" mother at age 52, and his dear wife Joy at age 62. C.S. died three years after his wife's death of renal failure. C.S. grew stronger in various ways after each painful death, and thus his quote we began this chapter with, "Pain is God's megaphone to rouse a deaf world." Is it any wonder that it became one of C.S. Lewis's best-known quotes?

Following are some of my favorite C.S. Lewis quotes, and meditating briefly on each of these will give you a beautiful view of how C.S. experienced God and God's relationship with his children outside the box.

In my opinion, the views of C.S. Lewis are "outside the box" of normal human intellect or reasoning about God, us, our relationship to him, and our relationship to each other. (Note: For hundreds of C.S. Lewis quotes I suggest obtaining the tweets of those quotes from @CSLewisDaily. Of course, reading his books is my highest recommendation, or seeing the movies based on some of his books.)

The Nature of God and His Relationship with Us

"Christianity if false is of no importance, and if true, of infinite importance; the only thing it can't be is moderately important."

"Christianity seems at first to be about morality, rules, guilt and virtue, yet it leads you out of that, into something beyond."

"Christians are the physical organism through which Christ acts ... His fingers and muscles, the cells of His body."

"You must ask for God's help ... after each failure, ask forgiveness, pick yourself up."

"Dear God, lighten my load or strengthen my back."

"God cannot give us happiness and peace apart from himself because it is not there. There is no such thing."

"If you are thinking of becoming a Christian, I warn you, you are embarking on something which will take the whole of you."

"Aim at heaven and you will get earth thrown in. Aim at earth and you get neither."

"God, who foresaw your tribulation, has specially armed you to go through it, not without pain but without stain."

"Faith is the art of holding on to things in spite of your changing moods and circumstances."

"When all the suns and nebulae have passed away, each one of you will still be alive."

"Try to exclude the possibility of suffering and you find that you have excluded life itself."

"Your real, new self will not come as long as you are looking for it. It will come when you are looking for Him."

"Whether we like it or not, God intends to give us what we need, not what we now think we want."

"We have not the slightest notion of the tremendous thing He means to make of us."

"The fact that our heart yearns for something Earth can't supply is proof that Heaven must be our home."

"The question is not what we intended ourselves to be, but what He intended us to be when He made us."

"He who has God and everything else has no more than he who has God only."

"If we only have the will to walk, then God is pleased with our stumbles"

"We are not necessarily doubting that God will do the best for us; we are wondering how painful the best will turn out to be."

"You thought you were being made into a little cottage but He is building a palace. He intends to live in it Himself."

"What God does for us, He does in us."

"The Present is the point at which time touches eternity."

"When Christ died, He died for you individually just as much as if you'd been the only person in the world."

"No great wisdom can be reached without sacrifice."

"Here is joy that cannot be shaken. Our light can swallow up your darkness: but your darkness cannot now infect our light."

"There are two kinds of people: those who say to God, "Thy will be done," and those to whom God says, 'All right, then, have it your way.' "

"God has infinite attention to spare for each one of us. You are as much alone with him as if you were the only being he ever created."

"Once in our world, a stable had something in it that was bigger than our whole world."

"The Son of God became a man to enable men to become sons of God."

"God does not shake miracles into nature at random as if from a pepper-caster. They come on great occasions."

"It cost God nothing, so far as we know, to create nice things: but to convert rebellious wills cost Him crucifixion."

"No good work is done anywhere without aid from the father of lights."

"Relying on God has to begin all over again every day as if nothing had yet been done."

"The more we let God take us over, the more truly ourselves we become—because he made us. He invented us."

"When we want to be something other than the thing God wants us to be, we must be wanting what, in fact, will not make us happy."

"It is when I turn to Christ, when I give up myself to His personality, that I first begin to have a real personality of my own."

"Whatever you do, He will make good of it. But not the good He had prepared for you if you had obeyed him."

"There are far, far better things ahead than anything we leave behind."

"What one calls the interruptions are precisely one's real life—the life God is sending one day by day."

"Repentance means unlearning all the self-conceit and self-will that we have been training ourselves into."

"You are never too old to set another goal or to dream a new dream."

"We can never know what might have been but what is to come is another matter entirely."

"All this trying leads up to the vital moment at which you turn to God and say, "You must do this. I can't."

"Our worst prayers may really be our best: those least supported by devotional feeling. For these may come from a deeper level than feeling."

"Obedience is the road to freedom, humility the road to pleasure, unity the road to personality."

"The Kingdom of God is to be realized here—in this world. And it will be."

"We are marble waiting to be shaped, metal waiting to be run into a mold."

"My idea of God is not a divine idea. It has to be shattered time after time. He shatters it Himself. He is the great iconoclast."

"We were promised sufferings, they were part of the program. We were even told, 'Blessed Are They That Mourn.' "

"Do not waste time bothering whether you 'love' your neighbor; act as if you do, and you will presently come to love him."

"If I find desires which nothing in this world can satisfy, the only explanation is that I was made for another world."

"1-To be God. 2-To be like God and to share His goodness in creaturely response. 3-To be miserable. These are the only 3 alternatives."

"The past is frozen and no longer flows, and the present is all lit up with eternal rays."

"Reality, in fact, is usually something you could not have guessed. That is one of the reasons I believe Christianity."

"This world is a great sculptor's shop. We are the statues and there's a rumor going around that some of us are someday going to come to life."

"The Christian does not think God will love us because we are good, but that God will make us good because He loves us."

"Though our feelings come and go, His love for us does not."

"A man can accept what Christ has done without knowing how it works: indeed, he would not know how it works until he has accepted it."

"Why do people say 'I'm not afraid of God because I know He is good?' Have they never even been to a dentist?"

"Either this man was, and is, the Son of God: or else a madman or something worse."

"Don't let your happiness depend on something you may lose."

"The sun looks down on nothing half so good as a household laughing together over a meal."

"The homemaker has the ultimate career. All other careers exist for one purpose only—and that is to support the ultimate career."

"Christ, who said 'Ye have not chosen me but I have chosen you,' says to Christian friends 'I have chosen you for one another.' "

"It does not matter how small the sins are provided that their cumulative effect is to edge the man away from the Light and out into nothing."

"I believe in Christ like I believe in the sun, not because I can see it, but by it I can see everything else."

"Getting over a painful experience is much like crossing monkey bars. You have to let go … to move forward."

"God designed the human machine to run on Himself. He Himself is the fuel our spirits were designed to burn."

"I pray because I can't help myself. I pray because I'm helpless… It doesn't change God—it changes me."

"You find out the strength of a wind by trying to walk against it, not by lying down."

"Free will, though it makes evil possible, is also the only thing that makes possible any love or goodness or joy worth having."

"[Right and Wrong] are not a matter of mere taste and opinion any more than the multiplication table."

"Hell begins with a grumbling mood, always complaining, always blaming others."

"Atheism turns out to be too simple. If the whole universe has no meaning, we should never have found out that it has no meaning."

"No man can be an exile if he remembers that all the world is one city."

"In science we have been reading only the notes to a poem; in Christianity we find the poem itself."

"I write for the unlearned about things in which I am unlearned myself."

"Hardship often prepares an ordinary person for an extraordinary destiny."

Human Nature

"We are mirrors. Yes, we are windows seen through by others but dreams are windows of the soul into ourselves"

"Thirst was made for water; inquiry for truth."

"To love at all is to be vulnerable."

"A silly idea ... that good people do not know what temptation means. Only those who try to resist temptation know how strong it is."

"Human beings can't make one another really happy for long; you can't love someone fully until you love God."

"The most dangerous thing you can do is ... take any one impulse of your own nature and set it up as the thing you ought to follow at all costs."

"Friendship is born at that moment when one person says to another: 'What? You too? I thought I was the only one.' "

"If we are skeptical we shall teach skepticism to our pupils, if fools only folly, if vulgar vulgarity, if saints sanctity, if heroes heroism."

"What you see and hear depends a good deal on where you are standing: it also depends on what sort of person you are."

"Nothing can seem extraordinary until you have discovered what is ordinary."

"We do not want merely to see beauty, we want to be united with the beauty, to pass into it, to become part of it."

"The only place in all of the world where you can escape the dangers of love is hell."

"Humility is not thinking less of yourself, but thinking of yourself less."

"The more pride we have, the more other people's pride irritates us."

"It is pride which has been the chief cause of misery in every nation and every family since the world began."

"It was through Pride that the devil became the devil: Pride leads to every other vice: it is the complete anti-God state of mind."

"If you think you are not conceited, it means you are very conceited indeed."

"A proud man is always looking down on people: and as long as you are looking down you cannot see something that is above you."

"It is the comparison that makes you proud: the pleasure of being above the rest. Once the element of competition is gone, pride is gone."

"Pride gets no pleasure out of having something, only out of having more of it than the next man ... the comparison makes you proud."

"Surely what a man does when he is taken off his guard is the best evidence for what sort of man he is."

"Nothing that you have not given away will really ever be yours."

"Do not dare not to dare."

"In our own case we accept excuses too easily."

"Courage is not simply one of the virtues, but the form of every virtue at its testing point."

"Isn't it funny how day by day nothing changes but when you look back everything is different ..."

"No man knows how bad he is till he has tried very hard to be good."

"It's not the load that breaks you down. It's the way you carry it."

"When you are not feeling particularly friendly ... put on a friendly manner and behave as if you were a nicer person than you actually are ..."

"The Christian, trying to treat every one kindly, finds himself liking more and more people as he goes on."

"We live, in fact, in a world starved for solitude, silence, and private: and therefore starved for meditation and true friendship."

"Life is too deep for words, so don't try to describe it, just live it."

"To say the very thing you really mean, nothing more or less or other than what you really mean; that's the whole art and joy of words."

"Progress means getting nearer to the place you want to be, and if you have taken a wrong turn, then to go forward does not get you any nearer."

"The more often a man feels without acting, the less he will ever be able to act, and, in the long run, the less he will be able to feel."

CHAPTER THIRTEEN

How Our Gene Pool Distorts Our God-View

Today at 2 p.m. I saw a longtime client, a very happy and successful physician. He was feeling great, and he surprised me by saying, "Dr. Meier, it is absolutely amazing to me how much my antidepressant impacts my view of God and my view of life itself. I was walking up to your building just now enjoying the birds singing and the sun shining and feeling loved by God and at peace with him. Before getting on the antidepressant several years ago, I spent my entire life feeling unacceptable to God, praying for salvation over and over again, and hoping that one day I would finally feel saved and accepted by God. If I experienced a beautiful day like today in the past, I would think to myself that it would do me about as much good as a beautiful day during the sinking Titanic."

I laughed with him and explained that how he feels toward God and life on his antidepressant is the real him—not the one who was always negativistic.

You see, my client suffers from a genetic disorder known as obsessive-compulsive disorder. In very simple terms, it is caused by a serotonin deficiency in the brain. We all eat tryptophan in our diets. Bananas are high in tryptophan, which is probably why you never see a depressed monkey! Vitamin B6 transports the tryptophan across the blood-brain barrier into our brains, where our enzymes convert the tryptophan into serotonin, one of the primary brain amines in our brains.

It takes an adequate serotonin level to have love, joy, peace, patience, and good sleep at night. The fruit of the spirit is dependent not only on a personal relationship with Jesus and the spiritual disciplines, but also on proper levels of certain brain chemicals. That is simply the way God made us. That is why even proper nutrition is vital for knowing God outside the box.

Poor nutrition can greatly influence your thinking and reasoning abilities. When serotonin is low, we have feelings of anxiety, impatience, and irritability, and tend to wake up in the middle of the night and have trouble getting back to sleep. We feel unlovable. We get depressed and also become more self-critical and negativistic in our view of God, others, and ourselves. If severe enough, and some other factors are involved, a person will have lifelong obsessive-compulsive disorder.

It is really quite easy to resolve. As a psychiatrist, I can take almost any serotonin antidepressant (known as a selective serotonin reuptake inhibitor) and administer it daily at about double the dose required for depression, and the obsessive-compulsive disorder dissolves away so the real person can emerge with a normal serotonin level. You see, we have reuptake sites on our hundred billion brain cells to "suck up" the old serotonin from the synapses between our brain cells to keep the serotonin level balanced and replace the old serotonin with the new.

Some people inherit reuptake sites that suck up too much serotonin, causing depression, and—in some more severe cases—obsessive-compulsive disorder. The serotonin antidepressants merely block some of the reuptake sites so that the serotonin level can rise to a normal level. If my physician client lives a normal Christian life until he is 80 years old, but quits taking his antidepressant at age 80, he will, within a few weeks, go right back to becoming depressed and obsessing about whether he is really saved and have a very negative and painful view of life and of God. It is just in his genes.

Some mistaken Christians (and non-Christians) think it is fine to take medications for diabetes—taking insulin when your pancreas can no longer produce enough. It is fine to take thyroid medication when you develop hypothyroidism or other medications for other genetic disorders. But it is somehow a sign of failure to take medications to replace brain chemicals that are depleted genetically or for other reasons.

The brain is just one more organ, so why treat it any differently than our other organs. It is true that millions of people in the world take psychiatric medications who do not need them. Rather than resolving their spiritual and emotional conflicts, they numb themselves out and continue in their sins or unhealthy practices. But there are also millions of people in the world who have inherited low brain chemicals who spend their lives suffering needlessly because they believe it is a weakness to take a brain medication. What a shame. Even the Bible says that medications are sometimes helpful. "A merry heart does good, like medicine (Proverbs 17:22)."

Another not so happy case study is the true story of Rachel. Rachel flew all the way from Jerusalem to see me at my clinic. She had severe obsessive-compulsive disorder—very severe. She was 28 years old, a successful professional, and a wonderful human being. She was a Messianic Jew—a Jew who believes in Jesus (in Hebrew he is called Yeshua) as her Messiah and Lord and Savior. She was totally dedicated to God even though she doubted her salvation daily.

She studied her Bible daily but never experienced the joy and peace it should have brought her. In fact, she felt suicidal almost every day of her life since early childhood. After a thorough evaluation, I immediately admitted her to our Meier Clinic Day Program, where clients get seven hours a day of therapy and my Nurse Practitioner checks on her medications daily when medications are needed. Most clients who come to our clinics receive no medications, just Christian counseling and some nutritional recommendations. Those suffering from a debilitating depression receive antidepressants for about six months and then do not need them anymore. But those who have genetic brain chemistry disorders have to take medications the rest of their lives.

I started Rachel on a simple serotonin antidepressant and climbed up to double the normal dose (because OCD usually requires a double dose), and within three weeks Rachel was happy, at peace, at one with God, and filled with wonder for the first time in her life. It was a miraculous change from her perspective—a normal change from our perspective.

She returned to Jerusalem to her Messianic synagogue, where, unfortunately, her congregation was legalistic about medications and psychiatry. They were nice people who loved Rachel, but just ignorant of modern-day science in that regard. They told her she had to quit taking her antidepressant and rely only on prayer and Bible study, which she had been doing her entire miserable life.

If she would have called me, I would have urged her to ignore them and go to a different synagogue. But she didn't. She quit her meds, returned to her miserable and suicidal self, and hanged herself and died. But now that same congregation believes in the necessity of psychiatric medications in those who inherit a deficiency, just like those with low-thyroid hormones take thyroid medication to stay alive or those with diabetes take insulin to stay alive. The brain is just one more organ. They even pass out copies of my *Blue Genes* book, a book I wrote to explain all the main genetic disorders in psychiatry and how to treat them.

Tom and Jennifer were a pastor and his wife who came to see me for marriage counseling years ago. Jennifer was arrogant, condescending, "always right," critical, controlling, and often ascribed evil motives to Tom even for the nice things he was saying or doing. She accused him of things Tom would never do. She also thought nobody in the church liked her, which was actually very close to the truth. These are all paranoid traits.

Some people develop paranoid traits by experiencing a life of bitterness and making other poor spiritual decisions throughout their lives, but other people are born with a dopamine imbalance in their brains that causes them to have all these traits, beyond their control. When I took a thorough history of Jennifer's life and discovered that many of her relatives had various paranoid disorders, some even schizophrenia, I was convinced hers was more the genetic type of paranoia.

I persuaded her to take a dopamine medication, and within 10 days Jennifer was kind, polite, humble, loving, and realized how ridiculous she had been to accuse her loving husband of the things he was so innocent of. Marriage counseling alone would have done almost no good whatsoever. In most cases, it would have done well, if the paranoia were not genetic.

I saw another client earlier that same week who was born with a GABA deficiency in his brain. As a result, he had lifelong social phobia. He was extremely shy and never developed any friends, even though his own siblings were all quite extroverted. He could not attend any small groups because of his intense fears of interacting with people socially. He managed to go to church and sit in the back row to sneak out quickly when the service was over.

He somehow made it through school and college and even became a successful storeowner. But he worked out of his office in the back room and interacted as little as possible with his employees or customers. The only reason he got married is because a young lady in college pursued him and persuaded him to marry her. He was a believer, but his relationship with God was also distant. He prayed but felt unloved and unlovable, almost totally because of genetic biological reasons. One day he heard me talking on the radio about social phobia, and came to see me for a trial on the type of GABA medications I had discussed on the radio. Within four days on GABA medications, he was totally normal, mingling and socializing with his employees and customers and even attending his children's soccer games. He thought I had performed a miracle on him, but my miracle was merely modern psychiatric research applied.

Celeste was a loving, dedicated, married Christian woman in her late 30s. She and her husband, John, came to my clinic to see if they could salvage their marriage. Six months earlier, while on a business trip, Celeste had a fling with a stranger for two nights, then became abruptly suicidal and depressed and confessed her sin to her husband. He forgave her, and they wept and worked through it and seemed to have survived this crisis.

But then three months later Celeste did the same thing again. Upon doing a thorough workup on Celeste, I discovered that her mother and a paternal uncle both had bipolar disorder, a totally genetic disorder that shows up usually in the late twenties or early thirties. During her two flings Celeste began going through three-day highs by talking more and more rapidly, making impulsive decisions, spending more money, developing racing thoughts, and had tons of energy in spite of only sleeping about two hours a night. She developed intense lustful thoughts and urges and would have said yes to almost anybody who would have asked her for sex during her three-day manic episode.

After the three days were up, she experienced an abrupt dip into severe depression— sleeping too much, tired, anxious, weeping, and suicidal. She would have been this way even if she had not acted out sexually. After six days of being severely depressed, her mood returned to normal for the next three months except for the traumatic recovery from the flings she had three months apart.

Her flings were caused by the bipolar disorder, not by sin. She had no control over them. In less severe cases of bipolar, known as Bipolar II, a person would have some of those same urges and tendencies but have some control over them and could resist them with difficulty. Not everybody with bipolar has sexual urges, but many do. It would have been a shame for John and Celeste to lose their marriage and ruin their lives over an easily resolvable genetic disorder. I put her on Lamictal, currently the best mood stabilizer, and built it up to a normal level within three weeks; Celeste has lived a normal life ever since. But if Celeste decides at some future date to quit taking her meds, she will return to the same problems every three months like clockwork. If her husband had an accurate record of her day-to-day moods, he could predict on his calendar what date she would have her next manic episode.

You may not have a dramatic genetic brain disorder like the clients I discussed above, but we all have genetic tendencies. Three things determine how we turn out as adults: 1) Our genes; 2) Our lifelong environmental factors, especially our childhoods; and 3) Our choices, which are by far the most important factor. My purpose in writing this short chapter to this book is to shake you up enough to stop and ask yourself what your genetic tendencies are and how they affect your view of God and of life itself.

Just like different puppies in the same litter of dogs grow up with different dispositions, some more cuddly than others, some more dominant, etcetera, so children from the same "litter" of offspring grow up with different dispositions as well. Ask yourself what your own genetic tendencies are. Ask those who know you best and love you most to give you honest feedback on whatever tendencies they may see in you, whether genetic or otherwise. Then use these awarenesses with considerable prayer, and experience God more outside the box than your own genetics have placed him in. See a psychiatrist for a thorough evaluation if needed. Why waste years of unnecessary misery?

CHAPTER FOURTEEN

How Our God-View Affects
Our Joy and Meaning in Life

Can our true spirituality have direct and indirect effects on our emotional and physiological depression versus happiness level?

A s a psychiatrist, I get asked this question often, and my usual reply is "YES."

We see about 3,000 clients at Meier Clinics around the USA each week, about half of them for depression-related problems. About 80 percent of them can recover without medicine, but about 20 percent recover much more quickly with medicine, with half or more of that 20 percent having a genetic predisposition to depression requiring lifelong medication with an antidepressant to keep the serotonin and/or norepinephrine levels up to normal.

In the 80 percent who do not need meds, the chemicals serotonin and norepinephrine are still often somewhat depleted, but not from genes (see my book, *Blue Genes*), but from various forms of holding on to anger. Resolving those emotional and spiritual conflicts usually will correct the temporary chemical imbalances over a period of several weeks or months.

Getting angry doesn't hurt anyone if it results in the truth being spoken in love. But holding on to anger in the form of grudges or vengeful motives will continue to deplete serotonin from the brain, keeping that person in a state of depression. Moses commanded the Jewish people in the Commandments (see Leviticus 19) that when they get angry at someone for something that person did or said, go ahead and get angry, and go ahead and verbalize that anger, but not in a vengeful way. King Solomon, a thousand years after Moses, wrote in his Proverbs (27:17) that friends confronting friends sharpens each other's personalities, like iron sharpening iron when you rub them together with friction. Three thousand years later, the Apostle Paul, in Ephesians 4:26-27, said that we should go ahead and get angry when our boundaries are violated, but to get rid of that anger by bedtime. In Romans 12, Paul added that we should turn all our vengeful motives over to God, who will get vengeance for us if it is deserved.

Violating that simple rule in both the Old and New Testaments results in a depletion of serotonin in our brains.

Ask Yourself These Questions to Determine if You May be Serotonin Deficient

Do You Experience, for Two Straight Weeks or Longer, Frequent

1. Sadness?
2. Lack of motivation?
3. Isolation?
4. Emotional pain?
5. Insomnia (usually awakening at about three a.m. and having trouble falling back asleep)?
6. Irritability?
7. False guilt?
8. Wishing God would let you die?

9.   Thinking of suicide methods off and on?
10. Becoming actually delusional, thinking strangers are talking about you, or that you have committed the unpardonable sin or are impossibly unacceptable to God, or that people are videotaping you or bugging your phone, or are you hearing voices that are not there?

If you experience three or more of these for two weeks or longer, you are probably clinically depressed and quite possibly somewhat deficient in serotonin, and should consult a professional counselor. If death wishes or suicidal ideation exists, be sure to see an MD-psychiatrist. If any delusional thinking or hallucinations are present, immediate medication by a psychiatrist in a day hospital or a psychiatry unit of a hospital is a must before you act dangerously on false information that your brain perceives to be true due to a chemical imbalance of dopamine in your brain. The dopamine medications will usually bring you back in control of your brain within one to two weeks, but until then, your chemicals are controlling you and tricking you into thinking that you are in control.

Forgiveness (not condoning the violator, but turning loose of personal demands to get personal vengeance) results in the restoration of serotonin to its normal levels over a period of time—often weeks or even months. Antidepressants restore it to normal within four to seven weeks.

Running to your doc to take antidepressants without resolving emotional stressors or spiritual problems like bitterness would be a really unfortunate thing, preventing you from growing to a more mature and insightful human being. But inheriting a low serotonin level and not taking a medicine for it will result in long periods of horrible pain off and on throughout your life, and often suicide.

So depression usually does involve a chemical deficiency of some sort, but can usually be restored to normal by good counseling and also good nutrition. The essential amino acids in our foods are what the body uses as building blocks to build serotonin, norepinephrine, dopamine and GABA, the main four chemicals we need for sanity. Vitamin B6 must be ingested daily to transport these essential amino acids across the blood-brain barrier into the brain. B6 is a water-soluble vitamin so it cannot be stored in your body. You need to eat healthy every day. Your brain then makes serotonin and the other brain chemicals out of these. Psychiatric meds work primarily by blocking the "reuptake" sites where these chemicals get sucked out of the brain and are excreted in the urine. Antidepressants are called, technically, "serotonin reuptake inhibitors"—because they inhibit the "sucking out" of serotonin from the brain quite so rapidly. So then the serotonin that your body naturally makes from the essential amino acids gets at a high enough level to produce love, joy, peace, patience, meekness, long-suffering, etcetera.

On my website, www.meierclinics.org, the home page has a link to To Your Health Liquid Vitamins, which have most of the regular vitamins plus the amino acids and Vitamin B6 in them, to be sure you have the ingredients in your diet for good physical and mental health. This helps many of my clients to recover from depression without an antidepressant, while others still need one, since the modern-day antidepressants are stronger.

Eighty percent of depressions and insomnia can be cured spiritually, since buried anger (bitterness, shame, false guilt, etcetera) depletes brain serotonin. But at least 20 percent of people inherit depression or bipolar disorder or other brain chemical deficiencies that cause depression or even psychoses. These require lifelong medications or they are doomed to lives of depression and sorrow regardless of their true spirituality or quality of lifestyle. But the majority of depressions are not primarily genetic, but rather usually due to bitterness toward God, others, or yourself.

Bitterness is like swallowing rat poison and hoping it hurts the other guy. But really nice people stuff anger also. Stuffed anger depletes serotonin from the brain into the blood, causing most headaches. Migraine meds merely block blood serotonin receptors. Ephesians 4:26-27 says to go ahead and get angry, sharing it with safe people, forgiving (not condoning) them by bedtime, or Satan will hurt us with it. Are you having a hard time coming up with a solution to whatever may be depressing you? Could Jesus think of many possible solutions to any seemingly "unresolvable" problem? Of course! He is God! So just ask him to show you one of them. Moses commanded us (Leviticus 19) to share anger but not get vengeance. Solomon added (Proverbs 9) not to confront fools who will only get angry.

Beauty from Ashes: When we chat with God throughout the day, the Bible says it is like a sweet aroma to him. He breathes our affection into his nostrils. In Psalm 37:4, King David teaches us that if we delight in our friendship with the Lord, he will give us the desires of our hearts. I often wonder whether God grants us our own personal desires, or gives us (implants) desires from him so we then want and get them—or both. If God gave us everything we desired, he would ruin us and make entitled, narcissistic "name it, claim it" humans out of us.

I often pray that God will not give me everything I ask him for—only what would be good for others and me in the long run. God wants to give us a "rich and satisfying life (John 10:10)." Sin is pleasurable or it wouldn't be tempting, but ends in loss and destruction. With one hand, God leads us behind the scenes, without us even recognizing it sometimes, while holding us up with his other hand (Psalm 139:10).

It is hard to imagine God being so intimately involved in our lives like this if we had fathers or mothers who were not involved much in our lives. In Isaiah 61:2-3, the Prophet Isaiah promised that God would substitute "beauty for ashes."

Actual Case Study

A suicidal woman raced to crash her car into a bridge abutment, but her steering wheel locked, swerving her into a ditch, her radio bumping on to "Saved from Ashes." That suicidal woman got home after her attempt, which was blocked by God, with her phone ringing and her family MD on the line. Her family doctor did not know that this woman had just made a suicide attempt, but knew she was depressed, and offered to pay her way for treatment in my Day Program in Texas, more than 1,000 miles away. The suicidal woman, during three weeks of Day Program care, totally recovered from her depression, which stemmed from childhood sexual abuse. After her recovery, she began working with other abuse victims and left her teaching job to work for a well-known international organization that helps abuse victims around the world. Within a few years she became a leader within that organization. She then went to graduate school, and she is now a professional Christian counselor.

Paul promised (Romans 12) God would handle vengeance on our abusers if asked to, so give God the night shift to restore peace and joy. Don't stay bitter, because if you do then you are unconsciously looking for ways to get personal vengeance rather than trusting God to get fair vengeance on your abusers. If you knew what God was going to do to get vengeance on your abusers, you might even feel sorry for them and wish he went lighter on them.

I learned at Duke Medical School (Psychiatry Residency) that bitterness is the leading cause of death. Sharing appropriate anger with our loved ones increases emotional intimacy. Loving confrontation helps both to grow, like iron sharpens iron.

Remember that in the Lord's Prayer we are actually asking God to forgive our own sins in proportion to how much we forgive our abusers' sins. Insomnia is actually a blessing, helping us either resolve genetic serotonin problems or get in touch with unresolved anger or false guilt. Insomnia gives us special times of prayer.

The nutrition chapter of my *Blue Genes* book (http://Amazon.com or http://Barnesandnoble.com) teaches readers what foods build brain chemicals that help relieve our depression and anxiety. Bitterness toward ourselves also causes depression and makes us more vulnerable to physical illnesses as well. Don't lie to yourself and create bitterness toward yourself.

During times of depression, it is also very easy for us to become bitter toward God or even to have doubts about his existence. This happens commonly, even in the most devout of believers. Don't become overly concerned about these, but chat with God about them, even if it doesn't feel like he is there to hear you.

Depression is often called "anger turned inward"

Temporary anger will seldom hurt us, but hanging on to it is the leading cause of headaches, depression, and even death, by affecting our body chemistry. Unrealistic expectations of ourselves, others and life itself usually result in hanging on to anger (bitterness), causing bad biochemistry.

Bitterness causes adrenocorticotropic hormone releasing factor to leave our hypothalamus, eventually causing fewer antibodies and more diseases. Bitterness causes serotonin to dump from our brains into our bloodstream, attaching to serotonin receptors in blood vessels and causing most headaches. If you went to an emergency room with a migraine, the MD would give you an injection of meds that block serotonin receptors in blood vessels. There are many causes of depression: medical, genetic, marijuana, excessive alcohol—but the main cause is bitterness causing serotonin depletion. Low serotonin is like smearing dog manure on your glasses and seeing life as being even worse than it really is. Many people who commit suicide would not have if their low- serotonin levels hadn't deceived them into seeing life as hopeless.

Depression is always curable with proper treatment, correct meds if needed, and insight-oriented counseling. Matthew (Matthew 6:33) taught us to take care of things that happen today and let "tomorrow worry about tomorrow." Live in the present. Remember that the leading spiritual cause of bitterness is repressed anger toward, God, others, or ourselves.

Remember that 3,000 years ago, when King David was overwhelmed and depressed (tears, insomnia, weight loss, etcetera), he called on God, who helped him (Psalm 121:1). Bill Wilson, pioneer of the very successful AA and related programs, urged us all to do what David did 3,000 years ago—call out to God. Calling out to our Creator invites his loving intervention into our lives to relieve our depression and the depression of loved ones around us.

Men versus Women

There is a false appearance from research statistics that women may suffer more depression than men, but women are much more in touch with feelings than men both genetically, through the hormones, and culturally. Women are much more likely to admit they are sad and to seek treatment for their sadness, while men in most cultures tend to be more "macho" and hide their sadness. So I believe men are depressed more than women are, but tend to hide it.

I wrote an entire book on depression, called *Happiness Is a Choice*, which has sold more than a million copies and was revised in 2013. For further information on depression I would encourage you to read that book. But the purpose of this chapter was to give you an overview on depression and to try to help you understand how easily depression can distort your view of God and hinder you from seeing God outside the box. How you see God and your personal relationship with God is also one of the main things that determine your happiness level, so it works both ways.

CHAPTER FIFTEEN

How Depravity (Narcissism) Distorts Our God-View

"Right is right even if no one is doing it; wrong is wrong even if everyone is doing it."

—St. Augustine

The psychiatric term most similar to the biblical description of human depravity is "narcissism." It is the opposite of Christlike love and humility. If you talk a long time about yourself, then you say, "I've said enough about me. Now tell me what YOU think about me," you're a narcissist!

Being closed-minded would be a curse, condemning us to a life of ignorance and mistakes. But if we are too open-minded, people will throw trash into it! And narcissists have plenty of trash to throw into your mind if you let them. What are the odds that everything you learned from parents, religious leaders, teachers, peers, and your cultural traditions are true? Zero!

In many cultures throughout the world, actually thinking about and deciding for yourself what you believe is a crime that is punishable—sometimes by death. I would absolutely hate for anyone to believe the things I believe because of any fears not to. Expecting anyone too is narcissistic and evil.

Would you really want anyone to stay in a relationship with you who didn't want to or have your beliefs for fear of your rejection? Narcissist! Narcissists are people who think others exist for their own pleasure. Mates and children exist to make them look good in the community. Narcissists reject others for having faults, ignorant to the obvious truth that their own arrogance is much worse than the faults they see! Narcissists wonder why other drivers are on their road! They try to prevent you from entering their lane, or they go slow in the passing lane. In prayer meetings, narcissists, naively believing themselves to be more spiritual than they actually are, pray the longest dramatically. Narcissists habitually choose what restaurant their group should go to, tell them where to sit, and talk too long to the staff for attention.

As a psychiatrist, I always encourage clients to be themselves, not "walking on eggshells" to avoid displeasing narcissists in their lives. In reality, being ourselves, rather than pretending things to please others, will result in rejection by narcissists around you, thank God. Why would you want to hang out with people who use you selfishly and don't accept you the way you really are? Did you grow up like that? Oh! Narcissists think they are always right and you are wrong if you disagree. Therapists call them "crazymakers" because they make you feel crazy.

I met a man so narcissistic he had a fake handicapped sign in his car and took up two parking spaces in the handicapped zone! Spoiled, narcissistic children often end up becoming criminals, or politicians, or both! I also know many really loving politicians too. Many narcissists end up becoming pastors or missionaries or other religious leaders. Jesus spent more time criticizing narcissistic religious leaders than any other group.

Arrogant parents who are blind to their own flaws see them exaggerated in you (projection). So life can be great if we kick them out of our brains! We have a choice to assume our own thinking is always right—a big mistake—

or meditate on God's words daily to gain insight (I Peter 2:2). In today's culture, status is often based on sexual prowess, power, money, or fame. But who will be highly regarded in the Kingdom of Heaven? Those with childlike humility. Humility is something only God can determine. If we think we have it, we don't! If we think we don't have it, we do. I'm just confused about myself!

As I mentioned earlier in this book, in 1985, I was the team physician for a mountain climbing expedition at Mount Ararat, in eastern Turkey, with a team of climbers headed by moon-walking astronaut Jim Irwin. While waiting to begin our climb, I enjoyed meeting many children of the Arabs living in the area. They smiled and sang songs and were friendly to us, especially when we handed out candy to them. They had beautiful brown skin, like many Arabic people do, but many of them had reddish hair and blue eyes. I had never before met Arabic people with reddish hair and blue eyes in all my many travels all over world. When I asked some of the older citizens of that area how so many Arabs in that neck of the woods had reddish hair and blue eyes, they answered matter-of-factly, "The crusaders came through here 900 years ago to free Jerusalem from Muslim rule and raped our women all along the way, resulting in reddish-haired, blue-eyed Arabs all along their path."

Throughout human history, religion has often been a tool to manipulate others, condone our own behaviors, and even justify killing our neighbors. The Muslims took over Jerusalem in 1076, and eight crusades occurred from Medieval England (including what is now Ireland and Scotland also) to free Jerusalem and search for the Holy Grail.

During the Dark Ages, and a period stretching over about 1,200 years, the Roman Catholic Church tortured, mutilated, stretched apart, and burned anyone whose opinions about true religion differed from the views of whoever the pope was at those times, killing millions of people. The Muslim faith also spread by the violence of the holy sword. The communists killed millions in the name of atheism including some of my own German ancestors who lived in Russia in 1917. My parents were 10-year-olds at the time and witnessed their older relatives getting shot. Even early Mormons slaughtered innocent men, women, and children who were in their path and would not convert, at the urging of its leader, who heard "the truth" from a salamander, mixed it with Masonry, and founded a new religion. Of course, most religions think they are the only right one. Just in the recent past, even Hindus—who tend to be very kind pacifists normally—burned 300 Christian churches in parts of India that are still hostile to any view of true spirituality that differs from their own.

Sigmund Freud thought that religion was the "universal neurosis of mankind." It is really easy to see why he thought that. But he was also prejudiced by the fact that he was Jewish in an era when he saw his own father ridiculed and persecuted for being Jewish by self-righteous "Christians." But just because there are horribly narcissistic people in lots of religious settings does not prove that all religion is foolish or neurotic.

I have had many clients who said they did not believe in the existence of any supernatural being and would never attend any church because there are too many hypocrites and narcissists in the churches. I typically ask them if they believe in shopping in grocery stores. "Why, yes, Dr. Meier, of course I do." When I remind them that there are just as many hypocrites and narcissists in the grocery stores as there are in the churches, they usually see my point—that the presence of some narcissists in any philosophical or religious group does not prove that the ideas of that group are all wrong. Narcissistic scientists believe in gravity, but that does not cause us to float off into space. Truth is truth, and only true seekers find it—and never completely. No two people on planet earth have exactly the same spiritual beliefs, unless you put your brain on a shelf and let a narcissist manipulate you by agreeing with everything he (or she) says.

As a psychiatrist who has listened to the innermost emotional struggles of thousands of people over the past 40 years, I believe there is such a thing as true spirituality and that my clients who were truly the most spiritual were also truly the most loving.

As a psychiatrist, I have also experienced much rage and disgust, and sometimes laughter, after hearing accounts of narcissistic behaviors within religious settings. And I am continually shocked over the naivety of the masses in judging which religious people, and leaders in particular, are spiritual versus narcissistic phonies.

One thing I like to do if I see a religious leader on television is to turn the volume down completely and observe the body language. It is amazing sometimes. You can see the narcissistic ones getting all emotionally worked up, squinting their eyes repeatedly, moving their heads and other body parts dramatically—drawing obvious attention to themselves rather than to God—and you will soon realize that some of the most popular religious leaders are also the most narcissistic.

If six religious people meet to have a 30-minute prayer meeting, some of them may be very sincere people who desire to pray for others out of compassion and love. Typically they would divvy up the time and pray for about five minutes each, but if there is a narcissist in the group, he or she will honestly believe he is the most spiritual and will pray dramatically for 20 of the 30 minutes, leaving the last 10 minutes to be divided among the remaining five prayer warriors. Some people will think, "Oh, how spiritual he (or she) is," while in reality, whoever prays the longest is most likely to be the most narcissistic in the group. In a church meeting, some people are genuinely moved by God or by good things happening in their souls, sometimes even raising hands inconspicuously to God. But the narcissists are near the front or even in the aisles, raising and waving their hands for everyone to see how truly spiritual they are (in their own minds anyway) and distracting the others behind them.

I have met many wonderful pastors, priests, and rabbis over the years, and have been treated with great kindness in Muslim nations I have visited as well. But there are still more narcissistic sociopaths in full-time religious work than almost any other profession.

Many people decide what sins they want to commit, then find a religion that will back them up.

My own religious quest has taken me through many doubts and searches and observations and changes of mind over my life. I have studied all the major religions, but have also meditated on the Bible almost daily since the age of 10, and still do. I personally believe I have a spiritual relationship with

God through prayer and observation and asking for his help to be a lover of people. I would never impose my beliefs on anyone else against their will like most of the religions of the world have. I attend church regularly, but do not personally identify with any one "denomination."

Other common behaviors of narcissistic religious people include such examples as:

1. Praying over a meal in a restaurant loudly, for others to see and hear, but leaving no tip or a lousy tip.

2. Going into full-time religious work so he (she) can "raise support"—meaning regular lifelong monthly donations by supporters who believe in that narcissistic phony—so they can do whatever they want the rest of their lives at the expense of others, but sending newsletters to supporters claiming exaggerated accomplishments. Don't misunderstand me, please. I personally support some full-time religious workers who I truly do believe in, who I know are humble servants who love people and accomplish much good.

3. God works in mysterious ways, and I never rule out or rule in anything my clients tell me about their own spiritual experiences—but the narcissists nearly always think they have more supernatural powers than I would guess they really have.

4. Narcissists think the world revolves around them, so the church should too.

5. Narcissists are self-righteous and always right, while those who disagree with them are always wrong.

6. Narcissists get bored easily and gossip and pit one religious group member against another, especially against the sincere authority figures who are considered a threat to the ability of the narcissists to manipulate the direction the church "should" go in.

7. "Shoulds" and "Shouldn'ts" in some religions are often determined by the narcissists.

8. Narcissists are habitually disappointed that the church does not do enough for them.

9. Unemployed narcissists think the church should support them rather than pray for them to find jobs or assist them in finding jobs.
10. Narcissists corner rich and powerful people in the church setting and talk incessantly about themselves to impress the rich and powerful.

So now it should be easy to see how our own degree of depravity (narcissism in psychological terminology) can influence our relationship with God and our expectations of how God should treat us. If we want to know the true Creator-God outside the box, we must deal with our own depravity and ask ourselves how our own sins influence or hinder our view of God and relationship with God.

CHAPTER SIXTEEN

How Depravity (Narcissism) Affects the Relationship between Our Political Activities and Our Spirituality

---

"A lie gets halfway around the world before the truth has a chance to get its pants on."

—**Winston Churchill**

Some Christians think truly spiritual believers should not be politically active. We should only be busy with "spiritual" tasks. Other Christians think it is a sin not to be active politically, trying to make a difference in our world to make the spread of Christianity possible and to be the salt of the world. Neither group has a right to tell others what is right or wrong for them individually as far as politics is concerned. I am personally fairly active politically and even serve as a consultant to national level politicians, and even a few from other countries.

Various political groups often behave like some religious denominations, thinking narcissistically that their view of all things is the only right view.

In reality, nobody really knows what all the political views of Jesus are in our world today. We have to make the best guesses we can about what is best politically. I know conservatives who are devout Christians, and I know liberals who are devout Christians. There are some things that the Bible clearly says are right or wrong, and I do not think any true and sincere believer should promote political views that would obviously contradict Scripture, but that still leaves lots of room for guessing what views are best for God and man. We should love each other, regardless of our political view.

> *It's a jungle out there*
> *Disorder and confusion everywhere*
> *No one seems to care*
> *Well I do, Hey!*
> *Who's in charge here?*
> *It's a jungle out there*
> *Poison in the very air we breathe*
> *Do you know what's in the water that you drink?*
> *Well I do, and it's amazing*
> *People think I'm crazy, 'cause I worry all the time. If you*
> *Paid attention, you'd be worried too*
> *You'd better pay attention or this world we love so much,*
> *Might just kill you.*
> *I could be wrong now, but I don't think so*
> *'Cause it's a jungle out there.*
> *It's a jungle out there.*
> Theme Song from the former hit TV show *Monk*

Monk was, in 2009, one of the most popular TV shows. Being a psychiatrist, I loved it because it is about a top murder detective with obsessive-compulsive disorder (extreme perfectionism with obsessive thoughts and fears mixed with compulsive rituals, like excessive cleanliness, counting things, touching things, rechecking things multiple times, etcetera). He is also somewhat paranoid, believing things are worse than they really are, but he sees the seedy side of life, so his reality is a true reality—merely exaggerated in his own mind. His psychiatric illness distorted his worldview and political view, but made him an outstanding detective.

Politics is the process by which groups of people make decisions. The term is generally applied to behavior within civil governments, but politics has been observed in all human group interactions, including corporate, academic and religious institutions. Politics consists of "social relations involving authority or power" and refers to the regulation of a political unit, and to the methods and tactics used to formulate and apply policy. ~ From Wikipedia

I would go so far as to say that politics is the process and power of relationships between any two or more beings, including family, marriage, a dating relationship, friendships, and even a human/pet relationship. Sometimes the owner rules the pet and sometimes the pet rules the "owner," as seen in another popular TV show *The Pet Whisperer.*

The key slogan of The National Rifle Association is, "Guns don't kill people. People kill people." The same could be said about politics—"Politics doesn't hurt people. Politicians hurt people."

In reality, guns protect people, and good political systems do too.

One Nation under God

My wife and I watch the news and often grieve worldwide tragedies, but "Christ … is the head over every ruler and authority (Colossians 2:9 – 10)." We try to keep up with what's going on in the world, especially during times of crisis. Sometimes we feel powerless and afraid. During political crises, though, we try to remember, "The King's heart is a stream of water in the hand of The Lord; He turns it wherever He will (Proverbs 21:1)."

> *"When there is no guidance a nation falls."*
> —**King Solomon, 1000 BC (Proverbs 11:14).**

When there is poor leadership in government, government intervention often spells disaster. President Ronald Reagan said that the most terrifying words in the English language are "I'm from the government and I'm here to help." Reagan also said, "Of the four wars in my lifetime, none came about as a result of the United States being too strong." Reagan *also* said, "I have wondered at times about what the Ten Commandments would have looked like if Moses had run them through the US Congress." He also wisely said, "The government is like a baby: an alimentary canal with a big appetite at one end and no sense of responsibility at the other." Reagan added, "It has been said that politics is the second oldest profession. I have learned that it has a striking resemblance to the first." President Reagan said big government thinks: "If it moves, tax it. If it keeps moving, regulate it. And if it stops moving, subsidize it."

On the positive side, President Reagan said, "No weapon in the arsenals of the world is as formidable as the will and moral courage of free men and women." And when it comes to the relationship between God and government, Reagan added, "If we ever forget that we are one nation, under God, then we will be a nation gone under."

Narcissism is basically the belief that the world revolves around you—or at least should—and that others exist only for your own personal benefit and pleasure. Narcissism is the opposite of the Golden Rule, "Do unto others as you would have them do unto you." Narcissistic behavior, on the other hand, would operate on a different political philosophy, "Do unto others whatever you feel like doing," or "Do unto others what makes them so dependent on you that they will keep giving you power over them." The "Golden Rule of Narcissists" is "He who has the gold makes the rules."

There are hundreds of political systems that governments, religions, sororities, or any other groups of two or more individuals could operate by and have throughout human existence, such as democracy, communism, benevolent dictatorships, and hundreds of other political philosophies. But the purpose of this book is not to be a book of political science, but rather a book that protects its readers from the harm of narcissistic thinking and behaviors in ourselves or others. The goal of this chapter, then, is to give you—the reader—a glimpse of what narcissism within political systems looks like, so you can recognize it and protect yourself from it—including protecting yourself from accidentally or purposely misusing politics yourself.

Most people are either primarily assertive or primarily passive. Assertive means to stand up for your rights and the rights of others. Passive means to allow life to happen to you, and to be angry when it doesn't happen correctly. A healthy, assertive person, when lonely, will say to herself, "I am feeling lonely today. Who can I call or visit to fellowship with to cure my own loneliness. Or who can I develop as a healthy friend who will fulfill my need to love and be loved genuinely by someone?" An assertive person, when financially troubled, says to himself, "I don't have enough money to keep up with my bills, so what can I do to lower my expenses or to earn more money or both?"

A passive person says to herself, "I am lonely, so it must be the fault of my church or neighborhood or family. They are not coming through for me. They are not meeting my needs. How dare they ignore me and not call me or visit me." Instead of taking initiative and making friends, they become depressed victims in their own minds and lives. If financially troubled, the passive person will say to himself, "Here I am, broke. That is not fair. The government (or church, or family) should be taking care of me financially and meeting my financial needs (without me having to do it myself)." This is in contrast with the biblical injunction to help the poor. But we have to interpret Scripture in light of Scripture, and the Bible also says that those who refuse to work should not even eat. There is a difference between people who are poor because of unfair and unfortunate circumstances and those who are poor because they are narcissistic and want something for nothing and expect others to meet the needs they should be taking care of themselves.

As you can see, passive people are more narcissistic, although some assertive people can be too assertive and use their assertiveness to narcissistically take advantage of others. Most assertive people, however, are quite responsible and are respectful of the rights of others. Most are happy. The vast majority of passive people are self-imposed victims and are depressed, angry people. Without getting too personal, if you think about it, various political parties attract either assertive majorities or passive majorities, even though both American political parties have their fair share of good politicians and narcissists. Ronald Reagan was a good and assertive president who promoted patriotism and personal responsibility. But it was also a Democrat, President John Kennedy, who taught assertive responsibility in his famous quote, "Ask not what your country can do for you. Ask what you can do for your country." So it is prejudicial to think either party is the sole possessor of righteousness.

In human relationships, there is often a persecutor/victim relationship. Being an authority figure within a family does not make that person evil or a persecutor. In any healthy family, the parents have to exert authority over the young, dependent, less-experienced children of the family. The older the child, however, the more the freedom to choose. The test of a good parent in a healthy family is to produce a young adult, by the end of the teen years, who no longer needs you to exert any authority over him or her. The healthy young adult now is the ruler of self, operating within all the political systems she chooses for herself, including the politics of her college, job, religion, and all her other chosen human relationships.

As a psychiatrist who has been practicing psychiatry for several decades now, and who has exerted an international influence—minor as it may be—to protect people around the globe by using books, teaching, therapy, and the media, I love politics when it is used properly and with love. Since none of us is perfect, we all exhibit occasional narcissistic individual behaviors, even if accidentally. But a narcissist is one who habitually exhibits manipulative and harmful behaviors, whether he is aware of them or not.

In a sense, you even have a political system set up to operate various aspects of yourself. If you beat yourself up verbally every time you make a mistake, for example, you are both the persecutor and the victim. Helping my clients become aware of the lies they operate on and to make choices to break those bad habits greatly enhances their quality of life.

In the media, we often hear about the horrible revelations of misused politics and the narcissistic and harmful behaviors of politicians. It is easy to get cynical and to start thinking that all politicians are crooks. Even President Richard Nixon, who made the phrase popular, "I am not a crook," was almost certainly not all morally black or white. We are all various shades of gray, some more shady than others. He probably had many good intentions and definitely made some wonderful contributions to protect American citizens, but he also narcissistically fell into the trap of placing himself above the rules everyone else was supposed to operate on. And then, after lying in the Watergate incident, which got him impeached, he operated on a self-defeating internal political system within his own brain. If he would have confessed his crime immediately, people might have been more likely to forgive him and probably avoid impeachment.

People tend to be gracious and forgiving to other people who admit their human failures, because humble people know we all have experienced personal failures from time to time. It is interesting to note that in any culture, subgroups of people operate under different "rules" of that culture. Throughout human history, it seems to me that men have quite obviously been treated more favorably than women. All races tend to have prejudices against other races, or sometimes even against themselves. Politically in America, the media tends to treat liberals more favorably than conservatives. But whether you happen to be Republican, Democrat, or Independent, we hope you do not condone narcissistic political actions by anyone, regardless of political or philosophical persuasion.

Remember that any behavior within any political system that is selfish and harmful to anyone else, including to your own self, is a narcissistic behavior. If you want to be truly selfish in a healthy way, give up narcissism and learn to love and be loved by people who love you just the way you are, faults and all. This is the only true path to peace and happiness and meaning in life. Narcissists may rise to political, financial, and sexual power, but they are all miserable in the long run and all die lonely and painful deaths. People who love and are loved and treat others lovingly not only have significantly more joy in life, they also leave behind a legacy of meaning and respect to the loved ones they leave behind. Love will improve all your political subsystems.

We all also have a political relationship with God. For me personally, God is my master and ruler, but he also loves me and gives me lots of freedom to make choices. When Jesus rules on earth someday for a thousand years, he will be a benevolent dictator. He will require all the nations of the world to observe the Feast of Tabernacles, for example, and when Egypt refuses to, one year in the future, they will suffer a year of famine (Zechariah 14:17-18). But I am quite certain Jesus will allow the nations to make many independent democratic choices. We can only speculate many aspects of the God/man political system from God's perspective. But we do know that the more selfish and narcissistic we are, the more mistakes we will make in our relationship with God and in our expectations of God. That is another reason why personal spiritual growth is so important.

God and Politicians: In Habakkuk 1:5, God tells us that he is in control of the nations, and that we would be amazed if we saw how much. Pray for our elections. Pray for our politicians, both good ones and the corrupt.

(CHAPTER SEVENTEEN)

Finding God's Will for Your Life

Your Worldview

I tell my single clients that if someone walks up and says, "God told me to marry you," run away from that narcissist as fast as you can! God's will for you may not be a particular mate and a specific job in a designated city, but it is (Romans 8:29) to become more like Jesus—to "be conformed to the image of his son." Scripture clearly says it is up to you whether to marry or not, but says (II Corinthians 6:14) whoever you do choose to marry must be a fellow believer, "equally yoked." Abraham was called to Palestine; Isaac to Rebekah, Mary to Joseph, and Jonah to Nineveh, so sometimes God is specific about who to marry or where to go—it varies. Sometimes he gives us specific direction and sometimes he tells us it is up to us, but to choose wisely.

Throughout my lifetime, I have often guessed wrong when assuming God's specific will for me. I wish God would speak up to me a little louder. When I ask God to speak up a little louder, he reminds me to patiently wait and listen a little better. When I ask God to please lighten my load, sometimes he does, but often he offers to strengthen my back instead.

God speaks to us in mysterious ways, so I will never understand them completely until I get to Heaven, and he led me now to tell you so. God often speaks to me indirectly, like through my little Yorkie lovingly licking me when I feel sick. I was sick but encouraged. God's will for me includes becoming more loving, like my Yorkie.

Knowing you are in God's will feels really good. In Psalm 92:4, King David said he sings to God out of gratitude. Think about that—even if you are tone deaf, God listens to you with joy. Being in his will gives life a song. The Apostle Paul taught the Philippians and us that at work, we should imagine Jesus is our boss and do whatever we would do if he was our boss there.

Being in God's will means having a servant's attitude, not an arrogant attitude. The mother/baby relationship is the baby's worldview, which widens as the baby matures. Paul (in II Timothy 1:9) teaches us that God by grace offers to teach us his view if we accept it.

Please ask yourself what your worldview is. How do you see the world and your relationship to the world? Our worldview is flawed in some ways in all of us, yet it influences our every thought, emotion, and deed. There are seven billion humans on planet earth with as many differing worldviews, so the odds of yours or mine being totally accurate are zero. Most people are in a foolish rat race to prove their significance (as I mentioned earlier, usually through sex, power, or money) and don't take the time to reflect on their own worldview. "Life" is what happens while we are busy making other plans.

In I Samuel 4:10, Jabez said a prayer that God felt worthy to put in Scripture as a model prayer for us to learn from for eternity. God must have liked the worldview of Jabez, who actually prayed for God to expand his business and increase his wealth, and, by implication, to expand his spiritual influence for good as well. He prayed for God's hand to be on him and lead him and to keep him from doing evil deeds, since evil deeds all hurt someone. Jabez did not want to be the kind of person who took advantage of others or hurt others. It is a great example of how to pray for the will of God.

God leads every believer in ways that are unique to each believer. I have heard so many stories over the years from Christian friends and clients, some of which were rather amazing, but believable. Others were amazingly unbelievable too!

When Dr. Frank Minirth and I finished our psychiatry training, we had no sense of what to do next, so we prayed about it and looked at our options. Frank finished at the University of Arkansas Medical School, where he became the chief resident in psychiatry, and I finished my psychiatry residency at Duke University, so I could train under a brilliant and spiritual Christian psychiatrist by the name of Dr. Bill Wilson. While attending weekly Bible studies at the home of Dr. Wilson, I met another psychiatry resident who really loved God with all his heart and was a dreamer and an innovator. His name was Dr. David Larson and he became my prayer partner for the next 27 years until he died in 2002.

When I finished my residency I had all sorts of lucrative job offers, since Duke was ranked second only to Johns Hopkins and ahead of Harvard at the time in psychiatry. The year was 1975, and I found myself praying, "Thank you, Lord, for calling me into psychiatry," especially since I grew up relatively poor. But then I had another "God experience." Throughout my life, it seems that God often tends to wait until the last minute to call me to do anything, probably to test my willingness to change my mind.

A few weeks before leaving Duke, I learned that the majority of counseling in America was done by untrained pastors, and all the rest was done by trained professionals. So I felt a strong urge from God that I should decline the high-paying jobs if I could get a job teaching at a really good seminary. The same thing happened to my buddy back in Little Rock, Dr. Frank Minirth.

I asked my pastor, Rev. Jim Abrahamson, where I could apply for a teaching job at a good seminary and train pastors in the wonderful techniques I had learned that were also quite biblical. He suggested Trinity Evangelical Divinity School in Deerfield, Illinois, near Chicago. So I immediately called them up, and they said to me that Dr. Ken Kantzer was the academic dean at that time. They gave me his home number and said to go ahead and call him at home—that he wouldn't mind at all—so I did. I told him, "Hi, my name is Paul Meier, and I am a Christian psychiatrist who will graduate in a few weeks from Duke University. I feel like God wants me to teach at a seminary, because I could help many thousands of people to get the right kind of help that way, by training pastors to do most of the counseling, rather than to just see a couple of thousand patients myself in my whole lifetime."

"You probably won't believe this, Paul," Dr. Kantzer replied, "but I was just on my knees this very moment praying that God would somehow send us a Christian psychiatrist to teach here. It doesn't mean you have the job yet, but the timing is so strange that we are definitely interested in you. When can you come for an interview by our faculty."

Needless to say, I was there in a day or two, and since I had studied the Bible all my life since age 10, I answered each of their theological questions with multiple passages of Scripture by memory, even on some obscure items. I was there teaching full time a few weeks later and taking seminary courses myself so I could eventually get a seminary degree.

Paul Little, who had written many books, including *How To Give Away Your Faith*, had an office next to mine, and I was very impressed with him and Gleason Archer and John Woodbridge and the many other godly men and women there, including Dr. Kantzer. Dr. Gary Collins was the head of the psychology department there, and he taught me a great deal also.

But they were only paying me $14,000 a year, and I had a lucrative offer to help run a large clinic nearby. I wanted very badly to accept that offer and be able to buy a nice home on Lake Michigan, rather than renting the small place we were then living in. Just when I was preparing to tell Trinity my decision to leave, Paul Little died in a car wreck. Dr. Leighton Ford, Billy Graham's brother-in-law, preached at Paul Little's funeral.

I was sad, but felt fine about my impending decision until Leighton Ford, in the middle of his sermon, seemed to look me right in the eyes and said, "When you are old and look back at your life, what do you want to see? Do you want to see how much money you have earned? Or would you rather look back, like Paul Little can from Heaven today, and see how you have been a pioneer for Christ?"

I felt God's spiritual dagger stick into my gut, and felt certain God was calling me to go to Dallas Theological Seminary, where they didn't have a Christian counseling department yet, so I could be a pioneer for Jesus like Paul Little was. I called Dallas Seminary and was accepted to teach there after an interview, where Dr. Haddon Robinson, who had urged me not to go into psychiatry five years earlier, now hired me to teach at Dallas Seminary full time for a further pay cut to $12,600 per year. I taught there full time for the next twelve years, maintaining a part-time private practice to supplement my income, pay off my medical school loans, and keep up my skills.

I took my "poverty vows," but God works in mysterious ways. Matthew 6:33 says to seek first the Kingdom of God, and not to worry about "things" because God will give us the "things" we need later. Among my first students were Graham Barker, who became the leading Christian psychologist later in Australia; Tony Evans, who became a leading black pastor, radio host, and author; Abede Alexandre, who became a pastor and a psychologist and taught later at Harvard (he is Haitian); John Trent, who did seminars with Gary Smalley and helped write several books on "the blessing;" and, of course, my lifelong buddies and co-hosts on the radio, John Townsend and Henry Cloud, who are among the leading Christian psychologists in the world right now and have written many books, including the *Boundaries* series. I wouldn't trade my influence on these students for all the money in the world.

Since Christian psychology was a brand new field of study in 1976, with almost no books out on it except for a few by Paul Tournier, MD, a Christian psychiatrist in Geneva, Switzerland, Dr. James Dobson in America, and maybe one or two other authors. So Dr. Frank Minirth and I (he also taught there with me full time) had to write our own textbooks, since there weren't any available. He wrote *Christian Psychiatry*. I wrote *Christian Childrearing* and *Personality Development*.

Together we wrote *Happiness Is a Choice, Love Is a Choice, Introduction to Psychology and Counseling,* and scores of other books over the years. In hindsight, the best financial decision I ever made was to turn down the lucrative job in 1976 so that I could instead teach full time at Dallas Theological Seminary (where I finally got my own seminary degree at age 40) for $12,600 a year. The books became quickly very popular and ended up selling millions of copies.

Is it possible that God didn't really call me into psychiatry? Sure, but I had to make the best guess I could, and I still love my job and think I have the best job in the world. I would rather help relieve peoples' pain than be president of the United States or have any other job. Is it possible that it was a coincidence that Dr. Ken Kantzer was on his knees praying for a Christian psychiatrist to teach at Trinity Seminary the moment I called, at a time when there were only about a dozen Christian psychiatrists in the whole USA? Yes, it is possible that that was a coincidence, but get real! What are the odds? Slim to none!

Was God convicting me during Paul Little's funeral, when Leighton Ford made a plea to be a pioneer for Jesus? I think so. And how about Haddon Robinson hiring me at Dallas Theological Seminary, which was a big political risk for them at a time when Christian donors hated psychiatry. And how about the great students? And how about the books I had to write? In fact, I felt called to write this book after Dr. Mark Young finished a six-week series on the names of God at Stonebriar Community Church, where Chuck Swindoll normally preaches but was on vacation. I simply felt the urge, out of the blue, and finished writing the first chapter by late that evening. But I wrote the rest over a period of nine years, as new experiences and urges led me to write various chapters.

I believe God has led me all the way, like he said he would in Psalm 139. Please be patient with me as I take you back several times in this book to Psalm 139, my favorite chapter in the entire Bible. In that chapter, God says that he designed you personally in your mother's womb, that he was thinking about you personally last night when you fell asleep, and that he was thinking about you personally when you woke up this morning. He also says that with one arm he hugs you, and with his other arm, he leads you through circumstances that you have no idea he is even involved in, showing you his will for your life at least at that moment.

Psalm 139 also says God—yes, the real God—will think about you so many times today that you can't even count them. Can this all be true, in spite of the fact that you didn't feel this important to your earthly father and mother? I honestly think it is true. I don't even think it is a coincidence that you are reading this chapter of this book at this moment. I think God led you to read it as much as he led me to write it.

God's Will: Specific Choices or Moral Choices?

Some people think God will in every case direct a believer to marry a specific person, lead you to a specific job in a specific city, and choose a specific house or apartment for you to live in, etcetera. Other believers think God's will is only finding the right things to do or not do morally in your life. God's will is only a moral will and all the rest are your personal choices.

Both views are partially right and partially wrong. Paul taught us in Romans 8:29 that God's will for our lives is definitely a moral will to become more like Jesus. But there are many examples in Scripture of God leading some specific people to make specific choices in their lives concerning mate, career, having children, and many other personal decisions. But I believe that in many situations, God also gives us many potential choices that are equally good in his view.

There is an undefinable balance between God's direct will and his permissive will. I believe I could move to a number of different cities at this time in my life, or even different countries for that matter, and be equally in God's will at each, as long as I continue to serve him wherever I am. I was listening to Dr. Charles Stanley preach on television one time when he was discussing finding God's will for your life, and one suggestion he gave really stuck with me. Dr. Stanley said that if you are currently in God's will but suspect that he may be leading you into a different direction, keep doing whatever you are currently doing until God makes it very clear to you to go in that new direction.

So I may stay here in the Dallas area the rest of my life because I don't have any clear calling to go anywhere else, and I absolutely love doing what I am doing here now—practicing psychiatry, enjoying my life with my wife and family and friends, and writing books part time when I feel led to do so. My father retired when he was 80 years old and regretted it, so I don't plan to ever retire until I can no longer do what I am doing—I may just slow down as I get older. But my mind is open to whatever God may call me to do, even when it is time for him to call me to come home to Heaven.

A compass is a navigational instrument that shows directions in a frame of reference that is stationary. Use God's compass whenever you're lost. Sin may be fun at first, and is very appealing, but ends in pain for many and also leads to various addictions, but "wherever the Spirit of the Lord is, there is freedom (II Corinthians 3:17)." Sinning results in harming others, harming yourself, lowering self-esteem, bringing on depression, loneliness, and a host of other negative consequences.

Living a life of serving God and others, while still taking good care of yourself, helps others, helps yourself, raises your self-esteem, brings happiness, builds love and a host of other benefits. I feel so very blessed to even be in a career that enables me to devote my working hours to benefitting the quality of life of my clients. No matter what career you are in, look for opportunities to be a blessing to those you work with or work for. It feels so good to wake up in the morning knowing you can really improve the quality of life for others and dance with the world of people!

I think it is important to live in a world of Christians and non-Christians, and there is nothing wrong with having some non-Christian friends if you are a committed Christian. But we all tend to become more like whoever we spend the most quality time with, so choose close friends who will lift you up and encourage the avoidance of sin rather than friends who encourage you to sin.

"Ships don't sink because of the water around them; they only go down when what's around them gets in! Stay dry!" Bishop T.D. Jakes.

Drawing Some Conclusions on God's Will for Your Life

When people in the New Testament era became Christians, most of them continued in the same careers they were in before, and kept living where they lived before. God's will for their lives, for the most part, was to keep doing what they were doing but to become conformed to the image of Christ and to become a good example and a witness wherever their lives led them.

The greatest verse in the Bible, in my opinion, on knowing the will of God in your life, is Romans 8:29, "For whom he foreknew, he predestined to become conformed to the image of his Son." God's will for your life is not primarily who you specifically marry (don't be unequally yoked to an unbeliever), or even if you marry. He clearly leaves it up to you in the Epistles whether or not to get married.

The Apostle Paul was apparently a widower. He expressed a personal wish for New Testament readers to consider remaining single or widowers even as he was in order to accomplish more as ministers for Christ. On the other hand, Paul recommended hiring ministers of churches who were married and monogamous. Sometimes God picks out specific mates for others, like Rebekah for Isaac in the Old Testament. Other times he allows us to make our own choices but wants us to marry other believers who will not draw us away from him.

Sometimes God leads individuals into specific careers, like the Apostle Paul on the road to Damascus. I believe he led me in my dreams to become a physician and use it as a platform to minister practical Christianity to people throughout the world. My entire life and career were built on those two dreams I had the same evening when I was 16 years old, the night after I went to the home of Dr. and Mrs. Bob Schindler.

Sometimes God leads you to a specific city to live in, whereas for others he wants them to choose for themselves where to live but merely to serve him wherever they choose to live. So, right or wrong, my view of God's will for your life is primarily a will for your morals (Romans 8:29), not your specifics. And yet, for many people in biblical times and today too, God gives specific directions for specific reasons that are beyond our scope of understanding. Be listening for both his moral and directive will for your life.

I have one more concept to share with you in this chapter: If I happened to find out someday that all these things were a mere coincidence and that no supreme being was involved in my life at all, I still wouldn't go back and change a single thing. I can't imagine a life more fulfilling that the one I have lived so far. If I die tonight in my sleep, I will die with my dreams fulfilled and peace in my heart that I have lived to make a contribution to society, and I would feel good about who I have chosen to become.

CHAPTER EIGHTEEN

Experiencing God through One-Another Concepts

The One-Another Concepts—Either Benefiting One Another or Competing with One Another in the Silly Human Rat Race

To truly experience God outside the box, we need others to help us grow spiritually and emotionally. The Bible encourages us to speak the truth in love one to another. We are also to confront one another, rebuke one another, exhort one another, love one another, serve one another, confess our faults to one another, and much more. These are collectively known as the biblical "one-another concepts."

As stated earlier, there are about seven billion people on planet earth at this time, and to some extent or another, all seven billion of us, deep down inside, feel like a nobody and go through life trying to prove to ourselves and others that we are not a nobody. We do this primarily through sex, money and power. The Bible calls them (I John 2:16) the lust of the flesh, the lust of the eyes, and the pride of life. I call it the human rat race.

People who truly love people of the opposite sex don't seduce them. People who are bitter toward them flatter, seduce, use, and then destroy them. Proverbs 5 implies seducers want to prove to themselves that everyone is like them, so they "seek the precious life" to seduce and bring others down.

When sexually tempted, which we nearly all are from time to time, pray that God will help you love that person more, not less, so you won't be led into temptation! We were taught in med school that those who are never sexually tempted should go to the emergency room quickly because they're probably either sick or nearly dead! Even Job, the nearly perfect Old Testament saint, needed God's help to "make a vow with his eyes (Job 31:1)" not to look with lust after women. Even Jesus was "tempted just like we are, and yet without sin (Hebrews 4:15)."

When it comes to money, author and financial advisor Dave Ramsey says to avoid "buying things you don't need with money you don't have to impress people you don't like."

When it comes to craving power, it can be as simple as one person trying to control another all the way to manipulation of the world by evil political leaders using deceit and many other sinful behaviors and motives. I have served for many years as a consultant to national political leaders—even some from other countries. I have known some outstanding and honest and devout politicians who rule well and with good intent, but the other kind is very common.

We all automatically grow up with some degree of the human rat race ingrained into our thinking. It is simply part of human nature. But to reach spiritual maturity and to experience God outside the box, we must consciously become aware of our own struggles, especially with sex, power, and money, and then quit the rat race the best we can. We realize we will often slip up and find ourselves back in the silly rat race type of thinking, but we make a conscious effort to quit the rat race and replace it with the Great Commandment—to love God with all our souls, hearts, and minds, and to love our neighbors as ourselves. We don't live to win a foolish competition for significance tomorrow, but rather live to love and be loved today.

Matthew (Matthew 6:33) taught us to take care of things that happen today and let "tomorrow worry about tomorrow." Live in the present. Matthew taught us also to live for the Kingdom—using our lives to serve God by helping people and he will meet our own needs. We are all "needy." We are all tempted to use sin (anything that hurts others or ourselves) to meet our needs, but we need to let God meet our needs instead.

God's ways of meeting our needs bring better results and a clear conscience and more self-worth, without taking advantage of others (sin).

I think insecurity is a waste of time! And insecurity raises its ugly head in strange ways sometimes. At a prayer meeting, the least humble and least spiritual person attending is often whoever prays the longest, especially if praying dramatically. The least humble drivers are often those driving slowly, or even the speed limit, in the left lane, blocking those who choose to drive faster. The least humble among friends going to a restaurant often pick the restaurant, tells everyone where to sit, and gives less money than what's fair. The least humble people at work often get promoted because people often confuse arrogance with confidence and competence.

FALSE PRIDE? False pride can cause distancing in our relationship with God and with one another. I got prideful when God accomplished great things through me on a mission trip to Russia, but I had a dream where God reminded me of all my major sins (they flashed before me) and shared with me that he uses foolish people to accomplish great things so he gets the credit. I told nobody about the dream, but the next morning a mission team member shared that very verse during our devotional and explained how God loves to use the foolish to confound the wise. And it was a different verse than he had planned to share the night before. Two years later, I got prideful on a Cuban mission trip for the same foolish reasons, and again God woke me up with a dream where my sins were flashing before me, including new ones since my Russian trip. This time God convicted me with the passage of Scripture that tells us that God's strength is made perfect in weakness. The next morning, having shared my dream with no one, another team physician shared that very verse, reinforcing the fact that it was God who showed me that verse the night before. And he had changed the verse from the one he intended to share the night before.

There are about 10,000 verses in the Bible, so the odds against that happening are at least one in 10,000 chances. The chances of that happening to me twice by mere coincidence are 10,000 times 10,000, which is 100,000,000. It had to be acts of God. To top it off, I had a dream that my daughter's car would stop suddenly on a highway and get rammed. My wife and I prayed for her, but I was too proud to call her and warn her because I was afraid she would think I was silly for putting too much stock in my own dreams.

Later that same day, our daughter called to let us know she had been in an accident. She was driving her car down a California highway at 70 miles per hour when her brakes suddenly locked and her car came to a quick halt, with the car behind her running into the rear of her car. But nobody was hurt. It was only then that I admitted having dreamt that very identical thing the night before but being afraid to share it with her. After a car-flipping accident I had on November 15, 1989, Jesus humbled me and showed me in another dream to number my days (Psalm 90:12).

I got a call the next day from my mother-in-law saying she had been praying for me all week to not get hurt in a car accident because of a dream she had about the same passage in Psalm 90:12. Sins, including the sins related to pride or entitlement, are the most depressing occurrences in my own life, although I also become bitter toward myself at times too. I "wrestle" with God frequently about both of these character flaws.

So I often find myself thinking "rat-race thinking" rather than Christlike thinking. I depend on a variety of spiritual helps to keep me on track, including Scripture, meditation, and prayer. But I need others. I need to have people in my life who love me enough to confront me, speaking the truth in love, when they see me slipping into those rat-race patterns. That's why I will always have a prayer partner.

Years ago, I enjoyed being on Dr. Norman Vincent Peale's radio program. He authored *The Power Of Positive Thinking*. He loved

Philippians 4:6, where Paul encourages us, "Don't worry about anything; instead, pray about everything. Tell God what you need, and thank him for all he has done."

Psalm 139 says God designs each of us to be gifted at what he calls us to do, but not gifted at other things. I love sports but am "athletically" challenged! Eighty percent of adults hate their jobs (among those lucky enough to have one!). So what did God gift you in? Find a way to do it, and life will become more exciting.

When we take the time to analyze any possible sin we might be tempted to commit, it becomes easy to see that sins all end up hurting someone. Feeling horrible after sinning is pretty good evidence that we are true believers. But the loving confrontation of true friends is a must to become aware of our own blind spots. So hang around with wise and godly people who love you enough to tell you the truth about yourself. There is deceit in politics, religions, culture, and even in ourselves. Solution: Discover and "fix your thoughts on what is true (Philippians 4:8)." And we often need one another to see the truth.

Prayer-Partners—Two Shall Put 10,000 to Flight

In Deuteronomy 32:30, Moses wrote that with God's help, one man can put a thousand to flight, and two men can put 10,000 to flight. You and God can defeat a thousand, but if you have a prayer partner you can defeat 5,000 each. When I was a resident in psychiatry at Duke back in the mid 1970s, I met a godly resident who was also a dreamer by the name of Dr. David Larson. Well, he became my prayer partner, and we confessed our sins to each other ever since until he died of a heart attack at age 54 on March 5, 2002.

When we were residents together at Duke in 1975, my dream was to help Christians accept the practical side of psychiatry and science, including medications for genetic disorders, etcetera. Dave's dream in 1975 was to help scientists and medical doctors and educators to accept practical Christianity and see its value. At the time of Dave's death, more than half of the medical schools in the United States had courses for medical students on the value of spirituality—courses designed by my former prayer partner, Dr. Dave Larson, researcher extraordinaire.

When I found out that he had died, I was momentarily jealous that he had beaten me home to the presence of the real God. He accomplished so much nationally in the area of religion and physical and mental health that a permanent Chair was named after him in the United States Library of Congress beside the Chair named after Dr. Henry Kissinger.

When Dave died, after grieving awhile, I began to seek a prayer partner who could possibly take Dave's place. I finally chose to ask a Frenchman who lives in Paris who has three doctorate degrees, including one in psychology. I met him during my first missionary journey to France. Dr. Jean-Luc Bertrand, who had become a close friend by now, asked me why I would want someone from France—so far away—to become my next prayer partner. I told him there were three reasons. He lived 5,000 miles away, so I was less afraid to confess personal sins to him. He was a psychologist, so we could analyze each other to guess why we were tempted in some areas more than others. And my first prayer partner, Dave Larson, was such a godly man, he didn't sin very often, and it was usually me confessing to him.

I told Jean-Luc that since he is a Frenchman, he certainly must sin at least as often as I do! He let out a big laugh and said to me, "Paul, I am qualified. I accept." We have been prayer partners since 2002, and Dr. Bertrand founded and helps run an orphanage in South Africa that completely raises and educates 2,000 children, most of whose parents died of AIDS.

Another prayer partner I have had throughout my life has been my sister, Nancy Brown. She helped me found the clinics in 1976, and has run the business end of things all these years, enabling me to devote myself to clinical work and all of our various ministry opportunities. She has encouraged me when our ministry has gone through tough times, as all ministries do from time to time. Whenever we had a problem, she and I would connect, often by phone, and pray about that situation. We have often prayed the Jabez prayer together, asking God to expand our ministry opportunities outside the box, and God has answered those prayers. I have had other prayer partners also over the years, each making a unique contribution to my life. We have seen many prayers answered in awesome ways over the years.

Having a prayer partner you can trust and confess to brings about a level of comfort with one's own humanity and need of God in our lives that we accomplish a great deal more for him and for mankind. The Meier Clinics have had many ministries, including counseling, international ministries, the books to eight million people, and other spin off ministries like Women Of Faith, which we started under the leadership of our partner at the time, Steve Arterburn.

In fact, Steve and I did radio together, live, to about two million people a day, but when we did seminars to try to raise funds for radio support to pay for our radio expenses, we did not draw large enough crowds. We were very discouraged and feeling sorry for ourselves when Steve shared with me during one of our commercial breaks, "Paul, I have been thinking about hiring a woman author to speak to other women. They won't show up to hear us so maybe they will show up to hear another woman. I laughed and said we might as well try—and Women Of Faith was born. Millions have come to a relationship with God through our various ministries and spinoff ministries. And I believe having prayer partners is a big part of the reason.

One of the best ways to get to know our true selves better is by having a prayer partner. I urge everyone to have one. I believe it should be a friend of the same sex. A husband and wife benefit deeply by praying together also, but we each need a prayer partner we do not live with to admit everything to, even our sinful thoughts and healthy thoughts and desires as well. We help each other get to know each other and ourselves better and better as time goes by. We need to have one or more prayer partners all our lives since we will sin until we get to Heaven, so we can learn from our sins to avoid bondage.

Mentoring

To truly experience God outside the box, we would benefit greatly by being mentored directly or indirectly by a variety of godly people, including pastors, Sunday school teachers, growth group leaders, relatives, friends, or significant other godly people who take us under their wings for special guidance and wisdom. We also, in turn, need to pass that mentoring along, looking for and praying for significant others in our lives who may need our own encouragement or guidance or loving confrontation, especially over longer periods of time. I have had many mentors in my life, including Dr. Bill Wilson, a Christian Psychiatrist at Duke who trained me and discipled me during my residency in psychiatry.

My prayer partners have mentored me also, as we mentored each other. I could list many others who mentored me over the years, including Dr. Kenneth Kantzer at Trinity Evangelical Divinity School and Dr. Haddon Robinson at Dallas Theological Seminary, but you get the picture.

Truly constructive criticism includes three important factors: Truth and Love over Time. Speaking the truth in love over a long enough time produces growth (Ephesians 4:15). This principle was taught to me by two of the men I personally mentored, Dr. John Townsend and Dr. Henry Cloud, who are now two of the leading Christian Psychologists and authors in America. John Townsend was one of my outstanding students at Dallas Theological Seminary. I felt led to take him under my wings and encourage him to consider going on in the field of psychology to use his gifts, and he did.

Henry Cloud was a student at Southern Methodist University in Dallas on a golf scholarship. But he took a course under my guidance at a psychiatry unit of a local hospital, and I saw his potential and encouraged him like I did John Townsend. I later made them my partners, after their training, and had them come alongside me to do my national radio broadcast to two million people a day, live, which I did for more than 20 years. When I retired from doing that, they did it without me and continue to have a national ministry at the time of my writing of this book. When people ask me which of my books would help them most with conflicts, I defer them to the *Boundaries* series by Drs. Townsend and Cloud.

While teaching at Trinity Seminary, I had an outstanding student I felt drawn to help and disciple by the name of Graham Barker, an Australian. I spent a great deal of time mentoring him, then later helped pay for his education to become a PhD in psychology. I also trained him more after he got his degree before he returned to Australia, where he has had a national ministry there, much like my own here in America, teaching Christian psychology through books, radio, and television ministries, teaching at universities and seminaries, and working with Christian organizations throughout the world.

At Dallas Seminary I also had an outstanding student who had great character and aced all my tests in spite of obtaining most of his education prior to seminary in Haiti, since he was a native Haitian. His name is Abede Alexandre. After mentoring him for several years, I also helped pay his way through his doctorate in psychology, trained him at one of our clinics after his doctorate, and then he went on to teach at Harvard for several years before narrowing his ministry to writing, private practice, and the full-time pastoring of a church in the Boston area where he delivers three sermons every Sunday: one in English, one in French, and one in the Creole language of Haiti, since there are many Haitians living in the area. The Meier Clinics are a national chain of nonprofit Christian counseling clinics, and now Dr. Abede Alexandre sits on our board of directors serving as one of my own "bosses."

I also met Tony Evans decades ago when I was a professor at Dallas Theological Seminary and he was one of my top students, getting 100 percent on every test I ever gave him. He also had great character, and I felt led by God to take Tony aside and mentor him. We got together for lunch at a Chinese restaurant on most Thursdays for the next three years so I could teach him Christian psychology to add that perspective to his theological education on his way to a doctorate in Theology. Tony is an African-American, but I chose him because of his wisdom and character, not because of his color of skin. He became one of the greatest pastors in America, and his sermons are still among the best I have ever heard, and my own pastors have included Rick Warren, Chuck Swindoll, and Dr. Jack Graham. Dr. Tony Evans currently has a national radio ministry, writes books, pastors a megachurch, and mentors other Christian leaders from around the world.

Tony Evans Quotes on the Nature of God and His Relationship With Us

"Coincidence is when God chooses to remain anonymous."

"The baby in the manger made His mother."

"Your view of a tall building is different from an airplane than it is from the ground, so try to see things from God's perspective."

"If you want to run your own world, go make one. God is in charge of this one."

"God never said that the kingdom life would be easy. He just said that it would be worth it".

"God will meet you where you are in order to take you to where He wants you to be."

"God puts dreams in your heart that are bigger than you so that you will rely on Him and His power."

"Stop focusing on what you can't do. Start focusing on what God CAN do."

"You can overcome because He overcame."

"Meditation means to hang out with the truth."

"Be careful not to settle for church and miss the Savior."

"If you are going to learn how to trust God at a deeper level, you are going to have to go through a deeper trial. Trust the purpose for the pain."

"God believes in retesting until you pass."

"If life gets too hard to stand, kneel."

"Little did Abraham know that while he was hiking up one side of the mountain, God was bringing His solution up the other side."

"To worry about tomorrow is to forfeit your peace today. Trust in God and rest."

"God can make the rest of your days be the best of your days. Hope in him."

"It's about relationship, not religion."

"God knows. God sees. God hears. God cares."

"When God delays, he always delays for a greater purpose."

"You will never discover that God is all you need until you get to the place where God is all you have."

"God will either give you what you ask for, or He will give you the strength to deal with what He wants."

"One of our problems today is that we have too many Christians who want God to get them to heaven but who do not want God to own them on earth."

"God is looking for servants, not celebrities."

"It's 'yea, though I walk through the valley.' Not 'yea, when I sit down and whine in the valley.' Keep walking."

Tony Evans Quotes on Human Nature

"Singles, don't marry the person you can live with ... marry the person you can't live without."

"Married couples, don't talk about a trade-in when what you need is a tune-up ... fight for your family!"

"Brokenness is often the road to breakthrough. Hang in there."

"A real man treats his lady the same way he wants another man to treat his daughter."

"A valley is but a mountain waiting to happen."

"Where you come from does not determine where you are going."

"America: Land of the free because of the brave."

"Peace doesn't mean that you will not have problems. Peace means that your problems will not have you."

"Insisting on living in your past will kill your future."

There have been others also whom I have mentored or who have mentored me, but I think you get the picture. There is strength in discipleship. There is strength in encouraging people, even if for a moment. When I was 13 years old I was planning on becoming a carpenter like my father. But Mrs. Arnold, a widow lady in our church who was in her 80s, was a real prayer warrior, and she always waved to me and said hi when we happened to pass each other in the halls or lobby of the church we attended. One Sunday, out of the blue, she walked up to me and laid her hands on my shoulders and told me she was praying for me every day, and felt led to tell me that I was going to be used by God in a unique way in the future. I got the chills, thanked her, then put her statement in the back of my mind and did not remember it again until years later when God was directing my career into one as a pioneer to develop a new field called Christian Psychology, which did not really exist to any extent yet at the time.

So no matter what direction your life has taken, you can be an inspiration to someone today. It may be momentary or it may be ongoing. But look and pray for opportunities to shine your light on others, because it is God who gives your light the power to accomplish what he wants it to accomplish in the lives of others.

"How far that little candle throws his beams! So shines a good deed in a weary world."

—**William Shakespeare**

CHAPTER NINETEEN

Philosophical Thoughts to Enhance Our Experience Of God Outside the Box

"We make a living by what we get, we make a life by what we give."
—Winston Churchill

"God specializes in taking bruised, soiled vessels and making them useful again."
—Chuck Swindoll

"For my thoughts are not your thoughts, neither are your ways my ways, saith the LORD. For as the heavens are higher than the earth, so are my ways higher than your ways, and my thoughts than your thoughts."
—Isaiah 55:8-9

"You are the GOD who does wonders; You have made known Your strength among the peoples. By Your arm You have redeemed Your

people, The sons of Jacob and Joseph. Selah. The waters saw You, O Elohim; The waters saw You, and they were afraid; The depths also trembled. The clouds poured out water; The heavens rumbled; Also, Your arrows flashed back and forth. The voice of Your thunder rolled along; Lightnings lit up the world; The earth trembled and shook. Your way was in the sea, And Your path in the great waters, And Your footsteps were not known."

—King David (Psalms 77:14-19)

Philosophy: The study of the fundamental nature of existence and reality in the universe, including the actual relationship between God and mankind.

—Paul Meier, MD

Philosophy is the study of general and fundamental problems, such as those connected with reality, existence, knowledge, values, reason, mind, and language.

—Wikipedia

The fundamental problems addressed in this book are:

1. What is the Creator of the Universe really like and how does that Creator think, feel, and behave?

2. What is mankind really like, and how and what do people really think and feel on the deeper levels of consciousness? With God, all things are possible, but because we are human, many things are highly unlikely! The wisest are those who realize how little they know. "Fools think their own way is right, but the wise listen to others (Proverbs 12:15)."

3. "Conscious" is what we think and feel and are aware of. The "subconscious" is what we think and feel that is just below our awareness but can be brought to our awareness easily. And the "unconscious" refers to our deepest levels of thoughts, feelings, and motives that we are not at all aware of and can only be brought to our

awareness with external insights from God or humans who analyze us more accurately than we see ourselves. We fear specific things we are aware of fearing. But "angst" (true anxiety) is our unconscious fear of becoming aware of our own unconscious thoughts, feelings, and motives. It is a state of a deeper sense of uneasiness that seems to be coming "out of the blue" because we, as humans, are not aware consciously of its origins. No matter how severe anyone's anxiety is, or how long they had it, modern meds can make it disappear within minutes, but only truth cures it.

4. Any wise and mature human will ask himself the following question: How much of my true self have I met so far? Whenever two people meet, there are actually six people present: the two as they see themselves, the two as they see each other, and the two as they really are. Only God totally knows and understands the two as they really are.

5. How does God choose to relate to us as humans he created in his own image intellectually, emotionally, and spiritually? Does God, in truth, determine how and where each individual human will spend eternity?

6. What do I, as a unique individual in the universe, decide to do with this Creator God? Choosing to disbelieve in his existence is a leap of faith based on unconscious needs to not be aware of his existence or unconscious rage toward one or more authority figures—rage that gets projected onto God. If we do believe in the existence of a Creator God, do I, as an individual, choose to ignore him, rebel against him, or grow in my relationship with him and yield my life to serve God and my fellow man as much as is reasonably possible? Every human capable of reason has at least temporarily made a passive or active choice about what to do with God. Since you are reading this book, you are actively searching for information to support or challenge your own predispositions about God.

7. Pilate, at the time of the crucifixion of Jesus, was faced with a great dilemma, and was forced to ask himself the vital question:

What shall I do then with Jesus, who is called the Christ? What will you do with Jesus? You have no choice but to make an active or passive choice.

Philosophy of Spirituality

"If I have seen farther than others, it is because I was standing on the shoulder of giants."

—Isaac Newton

"Instead of cursing the darkness, light a candle."

—Ben Franklin

Johann Christian August Heinroth, MD

Sigmund Freud taught that we are slaves to our "id"—our basic human nature. He did not believe in sin, but still was more or less saying we are slaves to our own selfish behaviors and thinking. Johann Christian August Heinroth, a German psychiatrist 100 years before Freud, actually coined "ego" (our conscious self) and "superego" (basically our conscience), and said we are slaves to our flesh (which Freud called the "id"), but Heinroth believed that liberty comes from God.

Johann Christian August Heinroth (1773-1843), a brilliant German Christian psychiatrist, not only coined ego and superego, but also "psychosomatic" (how our minds and our physical health are interconnected). Sigmund Freud, 100 years after Heinroth, based many of his findings on the writings of Heinroth, but is erroneously considered the father of psychiatry because he left God out of the equation.

Being a slave to our id without the existence of anything called sin or even of God is a very appealing but incorrect worldview. That is why people loved Freud and give Freud credit for many things actually created by Heinroth. Heinroth should be the father of psychiatry for his findings. But Heinroth was relegated to obscurity because he felt a relationship with God was a vital part of our healing and said we were slaves to sin without

God's intervention. I consider Johann Christian August Heinroth the father of Christian psychiatry.

Several Internet sources consider me a "founding father" of Christian psychology and Christian psychiatry, but I credit Christian psychiatrists Heinroth and Paul Tournier. Paul Tournier, MD, 1898 to 1986, was a Swiss Christian psychiatrist and international author of many amazing books integrating biblical principles with the principles he had learned during his loving practice of psychiatry. Paul Tournier wrote the foreword to my book *Happiness Is a Choice*, which came out in 1977 and sold a million copies. A modern-day updated version of *Happiness Is a Choice* was released in March of 2013. I also want to give utmost credit and appreciation to Christian psychiatrist William P. (Bill) Wilson, who mentored me personally at Duke.

My Personal Burnout

At 30 years of age, I was practicing part-time psychiatry in Milwaukee, teaching full-time at Trinity Evangelical Divinity School near Chicago, doing charity work nights and Saturdays, doing free counseling of seminary students for many more hours than I was supposed to, speaking in churches on quite a few Sundays, and "burning out for Jesus!" While suffering burnout at age 30 doing what I thought God wanted me to do, I read Jesus's words in Matthew 11:30, that his yoke is easy and his burdens light. When I learned at 30 that God's expectations were easy and light, but mine were heavy, I quit projecting my loving but fairly strict German father onto God and did less.

I discovered at 30 that when I did fewer deeds for God and learned to live a normal life, I accomplished more for God—his light burden and yoke. Some Christians got angry at me for turning down their requests to do the tasks I no longer had time to do. I also went through a period of false guilt, thinking that every need was a call from God. But I eventually got my life's routine in perspective and really did accomplish more for God when I slowed down than I did when I was a workaholic. It was rewarding to discover that God is not German!

Eternal Perspective

Dr. Scott Peck is a psychiatrist who became a believer while writing his national best- seller, *The Road Less Traveled*. Scott Peck's initial statement, "Life is difficult," in that book, is absolutely right. If you expect the rainbow you must also experience the rain. For example, it is quite difficult for me to obey God's encouragement to "always be thankful." Setbacks and rejections require an eternal perspective for me to ever be thankful for them.

I, as a psychiatrist, like to ask my older clients to look back over the course of their lives and tell me what was their greatest growth spurt emotionally and spiritually. In almost every case, it was during their greatest setback or rejection. Looking at their entire lives rather than the pain of a current loss enabled them to be thankful that they went through those painful losses in the past, because they find themselves now as stronger individuals than they ever would have been without that tragedy.

Dr. Tony Evans says that standing beside an enormously high skyscraper can be frightening and make you feel very small. But looking down at that same very tall building from an airplane flying over it enables you to have a true perspective of it relative to you. Dr. Evans encourages us to look at the tragedies in our lives from God's point of view, like the airplane over the skyscraper, enabling us to gain perspective and be thankful even during our times of grief.

Even in tragedy (including national tragedy), I try to be thankful for God's ultimate sovereignty. I look forward to spiritual growth now and a joyful Heaven in the future. Even if there were no God, living the biblical loving life—even according to secular psychiatric research, is still the happiest and most fulfilling way to live.

I sure complain to the Lord a lot! I have to remind myself to remember, "May I never forget the good things he does for me (Psalm 103:2)." We grieve our national deterioration, but are reminded (Ephesians 4:29) to still encourage each other and ourselves with "good and helpful" words. When asked about the distant future of the world (Matthew 24), Jesus predicted an increase of earthquakes, like birth pains (doubling each of the past 10 decades), and also more ethnic terrorism against each other! Life is difficult in our world, in our country, and in our own personal lives. The realization that life is difficult is actually encouraging in our worldview, so we will expect and grow from tough days and thoroughly enjoy our good and enjoyable days.

You hurt people, not help them, with expectations of no diseases, financial blessings without hard work, and things God never really promised! So in the midst of world chaos, my good and encouraging words are that, after many tribulations, the "good guys" will win in the end and Jesus will rule!

Sometimes I wonder how much of myself I've ever really met. The Prophet Jeremiah said (17:9) that we can't even comprehend how much we deceive ourselves—a frightening thought! The Bible says that at "The Judgment Seat" for believers, we will see ourselves completely, all forgiven. The song "Amazing Grace" will have new meaning. Hopefully we will be pleasantly surprised by many godly parts of ourselves we never really realized also and receive rewards for those acts.

Lord, my heart and spirit often wander and fail you, so please "create in me a clean heart … and renew a right spirit within me (Psalm 51:10)." Being a psychiatrist, I love the joy of helping people—"The heartfelt counsel of a friend is as sweet as perfume and incense (Proverbs 27:9)." How much power do we really have if we rely on God? We are empowered "to accomplish infinitely more than we might ask or think (Ephesians 3:20)." Having an eternal perspective helps me appreciate my day-to-day blessings in my career and in my home life. So hopefully my own personal worldview includes an eternal perspective.

Society Today Compared to 50 Years Ago

When I was a child in Michigan, farmers would set up a table on the road with apples, a collection basket, and a "$1 an apple" sign and leave it all. The farmers would pick up the money at the end of the workday. Do that in this era and see how quickly the apples, money, and table will go. When I was 21, an annual poll showed that 78 percent of us had "make a contribution to society" as one of our top three goals in life. See the newspaper *USA Today* each year for the results. The *USA Today* poll of

21-year-olds in 2012 had among their top goals sex without commitment, power, fame, and money. Narcissistic goals! Is it any wonder the teen suicide rate is 300 percent higher than 50 years ago? A poll of more than 90,000 teens across the USA by 13 scientists showed that one out of 23 teen girls will attempt suicide in the next 12 months. "Our Founding Fathers wanted freedom of religion, not freedom from religion."—(Ronald Reagan). But our teens today are growing up in a relatively godless society. When I was a senior in high school in 1963, I was the president of the Bible Club—and that was at a secular high school of more than 2,000 students. Now it would be illegal to have a Bible Club at a secular high school. The happiest teens in that secular poll of 90,000 teens attended churches or church youth groups.

I have the privilege of serving as a consultant to political leaders and their employees both here and abroad. Some great ones still exist, but they are the ones with deep spiritual roots. But there are still young men and women with great character in every generation, just fewer of them today than in many previous generations. A top general in the US military told me with tears of pride in his eyes about how his soldiers defended each other bravely to their death. Wounded soldiers are supposed to withdraw from combat to be removed and treated, but many hide their wounds so they can protect their teams. Extreme bravery, loyalty, character, and love still exist in the world, especially in our soldiers, but these qualities are getting more rare.

Healthy Interdependence on God

God guides our lives when we let him, lets us fall when we don't, but lifts us back up—the Lord "upholds us with his hand (Psalm 37:23-24)." Be nice to yourself today because "God, who began the good work within you, will continue His work until it is finally finished (Philippians 1:6)."

Fear of abandonment seems to be the greatest fear my clients have. It seems to me as a psychiatrist that the vast majority passively and blindly base their "reality" on fear of peer rejection—not on the truth! For radicals in many religions, the honest pursuit of truth that contradicts parents or peers can result in rejection or even death at times! As for me, I would rather be a martyr for the truth than a passive slave to lies! I have known Hollywood directors who have to hide their personal beliefs! It's almost funny (but sad) how those who are proudest of "open-mindedness" reject and ridicule anyone who dares to think for himself.

If Jesus is not God, why do so many people in the world hate him? Truly open-minded people can love those who disagree with them. But belief in Jesus will result in being abandoned by some. But God will never abandon you. "Don't abandon me, for you made me (Psalm 138:8)." God promised us he won't, but so many others have that it's natural to fear that he might also.

I love my life and love my wife, but losing loved ones hurts. When someone you trusted abandons you, grieve the loss, but realize that you only lost who you thought that person was and are now delivered from the abandoning person you did not really know on a deeper level. A pastor was grieving a church split until I reminded him that if he doesn't remove the weeds from his garden, then God will—so celebrate. If someone is a fake, then the sooner he or she abandons you the better off you are! Better sooner than later. Love and be loved by real people. God greatly desires for you to love and be loved—the Great Commandment—and promised to take the lonely and give us new families in Psalm 68.

Envy: Resenting that someone else has what you want affects your pituitary hormones, adrenal glands, and antibodies, posing a danger to your entire body. "Envy makes the bones rot (Proverbs 14:30)."

Daily Blessings

"The Lord will withhold no good thing from those who do what is right (Psalm 84:11)." God's love is unconditional, but his blessings aren't. When I survived a serious car wreck in 1989, I "reckoned myself dead," so each day since is a gift from God to be "alive to God (Romans 6:11)." It affected my worldview and my God-view. The accident caused an attitude shift that enables me to be much more appreciative of my daily existence and daily blessings.

Generational Curses

"The child will not be punished for the parent's sins, and the parent will not be punished for the child's sins. Righteous people will be rewarded for their own righteous behavior, and wicked people will be punished for their own wickedness (Ezekiel 18:20)." This is a promise from God. As a psychiatrist, I often see sinful habits of parents copied ("visited upon") by three or four generations: choices, not generational curses! Scripture, written by God's direction, never contradicts other Scripture in the original languages, and God is never "the author of sin." People, not God, invented "generational curses" by choosing a misinterpretation that gives them "power" to cast it out. Most people who cast away "generational curses" are good, loving but misinformed people who should still pray for generational habits to end. I saw a recent client who feared being cursed by his father's sins, so I showed him he cannot be punished for the parent's sins, according to Ezekiel 18:20 and numerous other passages of Scripture.

Denominational Sins

Denominations all have varying opinions on what things are sins, many having no basis in Scripture, like the absurdity that the wine of the Bible was just unfermented grape juice, even though the Bible warns us not to get drunk with wine. Jesus's first miracle was changing water to wine at a wedding. Even though salvation is a free gift of grace to all who accept it, if there are no good deeds that stem from it, it was not real (James 2:17). Radical religious zealots throughout history have killed "infidels", but, in Philippians chapter two, God says to treat everyone as more important than yourself. Legalistic Christians use certain denominational pet sins as ways to feel superior to others. Don't call anything a sin unless the Bible does, directly or indirectly.

Acts of God

Whether we favored the 2012 presidential election results or not, the horrible East Coast (especially New Jersey) storm was a permissive act of God and may have been a determining factor in who won. "The powers that be are ordained of God (Romans 13:1)." The hundreds of nations of the world have good leaders and corrupt leaders and a host of leaders in between!

God is never the author of sin, but even throughout Israel's history, God allowed both kinds of leaders to take power. We know from the Bible that nobody rules anywhere without God permitting it. God is in ultimate control, but how he balances those decisions is one of those things I will have to ask God about when I get to Heaven because I certainly do not understand how God sorts it all out. Being human, I get angry sometimes at the acts of God, but I trust in my heart that all of his acts are right and that someday I will understand how they could be. Experiencing God outside the box sometimes, for me, includes recognizing that there are many questions about God that I will probably never find the answers to short of living with him in Heaven.

The Apostle John said, "There is no greater love than to lay down one's life for one's friends (John 15:13)." Two Navy Seals in the seven-hour Battle of Benghazi gave their lives for their friends, violating orders not to, unprotected by overflying drones. In the middle of international chaos, permissive acts of God beyond my comprehension, it is encouraging to see the heroism that still exists in portions of our culture today.

Conflict Resolution

Sometimes I become selfish and don't even realize it. I may get into an argument and assume it is the other person's fault. That is just human nature. The main attitude God will have to help me have today is: "to do what is right, to love mercy, and to walk humbly with your God (Micah 6:8)." In conflicts, a mature person will "be quick to listen, slow to speak, and slow to get angry (James 1:9)"—an objective participant-observer. Imagine a conflict arising, but rather than overreacting emotionally, you "step outside your body," spiritually and analytically observing. This is an actual technique I use and get my clients to successfully use also.

It's actually amazing to discover how easy it becomes to resolve or remove myself from a conflict when I do pretend in my own mind to step outside my body to observe. As an objective participant-observer, we bypass past emotional triggers and "autopilot" responses to wisely respond more like Jesus would. When you do react spiritually, God will "delight in you ... quiet you with his love, (and) He will rejoice over you with singing (Zephaniah 3:17)." Imagine Jesus being so happy over how you resolve a conflict that he actually starts singing a happy tune to himself—and spiritually to you.

Nations have conflicts just like individuals do. Current worldwide traumatic events are scary, but God's personal peace is "a gift the world cannot give. So don't be troubled or afraid (John 14:27)." I often remind myself of the old country song that goes, "I read the end of the Book and we win!"—the last book of the Bible is Revelation. Revelation is the only book in the Bible out of 66 that promises special blessings and rewards to whoever reads it and desires Jesus's return. With all the bombings and peril in Israel, Jews throughout Israel have signs even on their houses calling for the return of their Messiah. I am a patriotic American, but my worldview places me as a citizen of the Kingdom of God. I would die for our country, but my greater loyalty is to the Kingdom.

Money

"Moreover, when God gives someone wealth and possessions, and the ability to enjoy them, to accept their lot and be happy in their toil—this is a gift of God (Ecclesiastes 5:19)." King Solomon taught us here that if God has blessed you with wealth, enjoy it, but don't live for it. Paul taught, "Don't love money; be satisfied with what you have (Hebrews 13:5)." How we handle money is an enormous testing of our character and flaws. I heard a comedian say, "I've been happy and rich, and happy and poor—but happy and rich is definitely more fun!"

In all this financial and political chaos in the world around us, I'm trying to practice "the secret of being content in any and every situation (Philippians 4:12-13)." When I obsess about financial woes, I remember, "What is your life? You are a mist that appears for a little while and then vanishes (James 4:14)." Life becomes much more bearable, meaningful, and often more enjoyable when we look at our lives through the grid of an eternal perspective.

When feeling upset by crises in my life, I often ask myself, "One hundred years from now (in Heaven), what difference will it make?" Solomon, after trying everything that sin had to offer, including great riches, concluded, "Fear God and keep his commandments, for this is the whole duty of man (Ecclesiastes 12:12)." Doing this brings love, joy, and meaning in life. The wise quit the rat race of living for sex, power, and money. The wise don't quit on life, or even success, but "fear" God (reverential trust) and live for a cause greater than their own narcissism—for loving and being loved. Paul said to "live a life filled with love (Ephesians 5:2)."

Psychiatry research shows that the happiest people are people who love and are loved by one or more others who love them just the way they are. Years ago the Assistant Surgeon General helped me gather data on happiness for a speech I gave to national level politicians and other leaders. Love is the answer. Research shows that in every major city in the world, the highest suicide rate is in the wealthiest suburbs. Love is gold; Money is fool's gold!

I think the suicide rate is always highest in the wealthiest suburbs because there are a higher percentage of people among the wealthy who spend too much time working hard to gather wealth and not enough time loving and being loved by family and friends. Perfectionists succeed the most and tend to enjoy it the least. Balance is again the reasonable answer. There is absolutely nothing wrong with being wealthy, but living for money and avoiding the love of family and friends brings "miserly misery." Jabez was honored by God for praying (I Chronicles 4:10) for wealth, but with God's hand of blessing upon him and for God's help in avoiding sin so Jabez wouldn't hurt anyone.

There are some very godly people who are poor because of unfortunate circumstances, or because they have chosen poverty while living devotedly for God. But the Bible says those who refuse to work should not even eat until they change their minds. "The one who is unwilling to work shall not eat (II Thessalonians 3:10, NIV)." Living for wealth is a sin, but equally sinful is poverty from laziness and dependence on others for things you could do for yourself.

There are twice as many verses in the Bible on money than there are on Heaven and Hell combined. How we handle money must be a very important factor in the Christian life. I know of one psychologist who asks new clients to bring their checkbook or a bank statement to a session for him to analyze the client by the evidence seen in the way the client handles money.

Research shows that those who reach out to others when lonely and earn extra money when broke are usually not only independent and responsible but also quite happy. Dependent people are very depressed. People who blame others for their loneliness or financial woes are very depressed. The love of money (or that attitude) is among the root causes in every kind of evil we do, since all sins are selfish and hurt someone.

God knows that some of us cannot handle wealth—it would go to our heads—while others grow spiritually and give liberally to Christian causes because of their wealth. Good "luck" today: "The dice are cast into the lap, but the whole disposing thereof is determined by the Lord (Proverbs 16:33)." Success is more dangerous to your ego than failure, so "forgetting what lies behind (past successes), I strain forward ... (Philippians 3:12-14)."

The Good Life

People often think godliness is boring when in reality Jesus said he "came that they may have life and have it abundantly (John 10:10)." Being a therapist is fun, because "the Lord has anointed me ... to heal the brokenhearted, to proclaim liberty to the captives (Isaiah 61:1)." Two thousand seven hundred years ago Isaiah already knew that God would forgive our narcissistic deeds by laying on Jesus "the sins of us all (Isaiah 53:6)."

Rather than the meaningless rat race of the masses, God urges us to dedicate our lives to the joy of benefitting our fellow man (Rom. 12:1). If sin wasn't so much fun it wouldn't be so tempting, but all sins hurt somebody, so God always places "a way to escape" them (1 Corinthians 10:13)."

Because of my human nature, I doubt a day goes by without me sinning in selfish thoughts or motives or deeds, but I learn and grow from them.

The "Golden Rule" is "Do to others as you would have them to do to you (Luke 6:31)." I've changed my mind many times when thinking about this. "If anyone would come after me, he must deny himself (Luke 9:23)."

We all have sinful natures, so it takes daily willful choices to do this. But sin depresses me, so life is actually much more fun and abundant when I decide not to sin. We Christians are far from perfect, but Paul said in II Corinthians 5:17 (in the original Greek version), that as new or old believers, "all things are becoming new." If I were an atheist psychiatrist, knowing what I know, I would still choose biblical principles to live by because they truly do bring joy.

David said, "Joyful are people of integrity, who follow the instructions of the Lord (Psalm 119:1)." So denying ourselves sin ends up bringing joyful lives. I told a client recently, "I'm very sorry you're going through this painful situation, but you'll become stronger than you ever were before." I don't wish for painful trials for my clients, but remember, "Rejoice in hope, be patient in tribulation, be constant in prayer (Romans 12:12)." During times when those I love feel like giving up, I know that "the LORD shall renew their strength"—like eagles soaring again (Isaiah 40:30,31).

I think we would all benefit from some professional counseling at some times in life, but it's great to have God as our best counselor. God said in Psalm 32:8, "I will instruct you and teach you in the way you should go; I will counsel you and watch over you." Sometimes God lets you hit rock bottom so that you will know that he is the Rock at the bottom. Ultimately, God wants us to experience the good life—the abundant life—even though we will all suffer from many trials and tribulations. I believe this to be a biblical worldview.

Some Christmas Thoughts

"How many observe Christ's birthday! How few, his precepts! O! 'tis easier to keep Holidays than Commandments."

—**Ben Franklin**

It's better to give than to receive, but receiving feels good too, and it should! Jesus did both. Don't harbor false guilt. Never look a gift horse in the mouth. A narcissist looks at the horse's teeth to see if the horse is as young as he deserves for nothing! When anyone gives you a gift, whether you like the gift or not, say thank you. It is the thought that counts. Giving and receiving Christmas presents is a choice for each individual to make for themselves, not for each other.

Christmas, especially Christmas dinner, is never the right time for you to try to "fix" your relatives. Love everyone there as they are. Be sure to share with your children the true meaning and purpose of celebrating the birth of Jesus, but let them enjoy all the fun things too.

The first Christmas tree was invented by Martin Luther, who brought one into his home because it pointed up to Jesus in Heaven and was a great reminder. In reality, Jesus was probably born in the fall, at the Feast of Tabernacles, but I think he appreciates us celebrating his birth annually, no matter what date we pick. I doubt if the shepherds were out feeding their flocks in the snow on December 25th of the year Jesus was born. John taught us in John 1:14, "And the Word became flesh and dwelt among us"—but the word for "dwelt" there is a Greek word only used once in the entire Bible, and the word means that Jesus became flesh (became a baby) and "tabernacled" among us.

Born in Sin

As sweet as babies are, our natures are narcissistic, but love and discipline (not spoiling them) brings them maturity, success, and love. King Solomon said that a child who is "left to himself" in his natural personality will grow up and "bring his mother to shame." Research shows (and Solomon said), a selfish parent spoils a child (probably to get constant approval), but unconsciously hates or resents the spoiled child.

Can God Really Use Me?

Only God knows the best of me and the worst of me, and I am sure I would be surprised by both. We don't know our potential for good or evil. Mankind has still not seen all that God could accomplish through someone totally devoted to him. You might become that person! If you understand your own weaknesses and foolishness, then the more weak and foolish you are, the more qualified you are to be used by God. God's strength is proven by using weak people like you or me, and he chooses the foolish people of the world to confound the wise.

Open-mindedness

If you are TOO open-minded, people will throw trash into it. Don't trust the "craftiness of people in their deceitful scheming (Ephesians 4:16)." It's fine and good to give genuine love to people, but never give trust to anyone. Love is a choice and a gift, but trust must be earned.

Situational Ethics

It's never right to do wrong to do right. Exceptions? Rahab the harlot was an exception, making the Hebrews 11 "Hall of Fame of Faith" by lying to protect Jews at Jericho. She lied for God and became one of Jesus's ancestors, the great-grandmother of King David. Does this show the grace of God? Choosing a gentile prostitute who became a believer and lied for God at the Battle of Jericho to be an ancestor of Jesus and a member of the Hall of Fame of Faith in Hebrews 11. Rahab is mentioned in the lineage of both Mary (Luke 1) and Joseph (Matthew 1). Boas was her son.

Coincidences

When we get to Heaven, I suspect we'll be shocked to discover how many "coincidences" in our lives here on planet earth weren't!

Blessings to Troubles Ratio

"I promise this very day that I will repay two blessings for each of your troubles (Zechariah 9:12)." Dear Lord, I think I have some blessings coming!

Dieter's Verse

John 3:30: "He must increase, but I must decrease." (Joking of course). This verse refers to egos, not weight!

Sovereignty

"The gate is narrow and the way is hard that leads to life ... and ... those who find it are few (Matthew 7:13,14)." None would seek to know God personally without God's enablement. Giving control of our lives to a supernatural Being we have never seen can only occur by Divine calling and supernatural means. But interpret Scripture in light of Scripture. "The Lord is not slack concerning His promise, as some men count slackness, but is longsuffering toward us, not willing that any should perish, but that all should come to repentance (II Peter 3:9)."

Christians spend too much time debating sovereignty versus free will when both are obviously true somehow. We are better off spending our time serving God and others and finding out how it all works when we get to Heaven. D.L. Moody wisely said years ago that on the outside of the door to Heaven it says that "whosoever will may come in," but on the inside it says "chosen from before the foundation of the world." How that all fits together Moody admitted he did not understand, and I don't understand it all either and simply, therefore, do not worry about it. I love and work beside Christians who are on both sides of that unnecessary debate.

The Sufficiency of Christ

Christ is sufficient to do anything and everything, but he still chooses to use people and even scientific discoveries to accomplish his will. For example, there are many cures for many types of cancer today that did not exist when I attended medical school. One out of every three people develops cancer at some time in their lives, so many godly believers are alive today who have taken advantage of modern scientific discoveries. All truth is God's truth. Christ is sufficient to cure cancer without treatment, but he usually doesn't. Everyone he healed during his public ministry died of something else later. The same applies to mental biochemical disorders. Modern meds can do miraculous things to restore people to sanity who would have stayed out of touch in past decades and throughout human history. I debated a famous L.A. Pastor who misquoted "My grace is sufficient for you (II Corinthians 12:9)" to mean no psychiatric meds or professional Christian counselors are needed. I told him that God loves this pastor's wife and that Christ is sufficient for her as well, so she doesn't really need him. But I said that if he gives his wife a loving hug after this debate is over I am sure God would appreciate using a human to do what he could do without that pastor.

Three thousand years ago, King Solomon taught, "A righteous person cares for the life of his animal (Proverbs 12:10)." Kindness extends to our pets too. God is sufficient to care totally for your pets like he does the wild animals of the world, but I am sure he appreciates your kind and loving care of your pets. He doesn't need you but he chooses to use you for your pet's good and your own good and the lessons you learn from having pets.

God is sufficient to keep your car running, but he expects you to use a good mechanic for the things you can't fix yourself or don't have the time to fix. You and I have more power than we can imagine. "The words of the wise bring healing (Proverbs 12:18)." Again, God uses people, even professional counselors, to bring healing. Proverbs 11:14 teaches us, "Where no counsel is, the people fall: but in the multitude of counselors there is safety."

People who have diseases, even diseases of the brain, need medications to live the life God wants them to live to serve him most effectively. Try being an encouragement to someone today in person or online and see for yourself who you can bring healing to. God can heal them without you, but he loves to work through his children. Paul said we can experience "but never fully comprehend God's love, to obtain fullness of life and power that comes from God (Ephesians 3:19)." Pray today for God's power in your life to dance with the world and spread God's love to others around you that God has brought into your life.

Unrealistic Expectations We Put on God

In Proverbs 13:12, King Solomon says, "Hope deferred makes the heart sick." Often we have unrealistic hopes that we have to give up to avoid depression. The reason that "hope deferred makes the heart sick" is because depression is anger turned inward, so deferred hope feeds bitterness and depression. Hoping you lose weight without exercise, hoping God heals all your diseases without meds or doctors, hoping God forces a mate to come back—these are all examples of hopes deferred that God never promises to do, even though he sometimes does.

If you assume God will deliver unrealistic hopes, then you'd better hope you listen if and when God calls you to give up your demands. God can do anything, and Heaven is perfect, but he promises trials in this life to all!

Charles Spurgeon

"Ours is more than mental work—it is heart work, the labor of our inmost soul." (1866, London Pastor Charles Spurgeon, to stir his students).

When I was 12 years old, my dad paid me 25 cents each for reading sermons by Charles Spurgeon, which helped me in both wallet and soul-growth. London Pastor Charles Spurgeon (1800s) founded and maintained 65 charitable organizations: pregnancy centers, centers for unwed moms, orphanages, etcetera. He was a prolific writer and had millions of his writings given out for free by Oxford and Cambridge universities. In all, 926,290 copies of Spurgeon's writings were given out by Oxford, Cambridge, and other groups in 1878 alone. They wouldn't do that in this era. Like Charles Spurgeon, I pray that God will enable us to not only use our brains, but to do "heart work, the labor of our inmost soul."

(CHAPTER TWENTY)

Salvation

|————————————————————————————|

W hen I was 18 years old I was a freshman in college and was very concerned about my friends who were already serving in the Viet Nam war. I felt pained that so many thousands were losing their lives and wanted to do whatever small acts I could to be sure more of those who died would go to Heaven. So I decided to donate several hours every Saturday to go to a Christian Servicemen's Center in a city near my university. There was a military training camp nearby.

At the Christian Servicemen's Center, the staff provided free food and soft drinks and some ping-pong tables for servicemen to come to when they had a break from their basic training. After feeding them and playing ping-pong or other games with them, our goal was to share the plan of salvation with them, if they were interested, and see if they would put their faith in Jesus to forgive their sins and save their souls. We used the "Romans Road" to lead them to Jesus: Romans 3:23, Romans 6:23, Romans 10:13, and then John 1:12.

In Romans 3:23, Paul said that all of us have sinned and come short of the glory of God. We are all sinners.

In Romans 6:23, Paul said that the wages of our sin is death—eternal death in Hell.

Paul also said, "For everyone who calls on the name of the Lord will be saved (Romans 10:13)."

Also, in John 1:12, John said that everyone who receives Jesus as Lord and Savior is given the right and the power to become children of God.

So I memorized these verses and had my plan for how to share the salvation opportunity with servicemen before they got shipped off to Viet Nam. But I was scared to death. I was somewhat shy, and the thought of sharing the plan of salvation with young soldiers was frightening to me. My first day there I went out on the downtown street in front of the Servicemen's Center to invite passing servicemen up for free food and games.

Being scared, I prayed silently before I started, "Dear God, you know how scared I am to do this, so please make the first one easy." That very moment, as I was finishing my silent prayer, a young soldier came up behind me and tapped me on the shoulder. I turned around and he said his name was David. I told him mine was Paul. Then he said, "I have an unusual request for you, Paul. I am finishing my basic training and getting ready to get shipped off to Viet Nam next week. I got a letter from my mom last night, and she told me to be sure to become a Christian before I went to war. Do you know how to show me how to do that?"

I practically cried with joy in front of him, but held it back, took him upstairs, and went immediately to a private area and shared the Romans Road with him. He prayed to receive Jesus on the spot and was quite relieved to do so. God had made the first one easy, and after that I was no longer scared, leading more than 300 soldiers to faith in Jesus over the coming Saturdays.

I think there are millions of people who have, at one moment or another, prayed for God to forgive their sins but have never made their experience known to very many others. I think we will be shocked by who we see in Heaven we didn't think we would, "For everyone who calls on the name of the Lord will be saved (Romans 10:13)." Jesus said that he has many sheep we don't know about (John 10:16). In Ephesians 2:8-9, Paul promises salvation is by grace = unmerited favor, not by any good works; a gift of God to all who ask even once in faith.

Whatever qualified the thief on the cross to go with Jesus to Heaven qualifies all—no church, no baptism or good works, just a moment of faith. When anyone does have a moment of faith, if sincere, more good works will come from it—all things becoming new in time. A wedding ring is a symbol of your marriage, like baptism is a symbol of your relationship to God—both being good but not necessary.

I was giving a speech once to a large group of Christians from various denominations, using slides for my speech. Unexpectedly, a blank slide popped up, so I spontaneously said, "This is a slide of all the verses in the Bible on infant baptism!" Since there are no verses in the Bible on infant baptism, I got quite a laugh, even from those who practice it in their denominations. The thief on the cross merely put his faith in Jesus, and Jesus told him he would be with Jesus that very day in Paradise.

I have been meditating on Scripture daily since age 10, and it is alive, with new passages standing out each time through the Bible and bringing brand new heart insights. "Heart" implies our innermost thoughts, feelings, and motives that we sometimes hide from others and even more from our own conscious awareness. In Proverbs 21:2, wise King Solomon wrote, "Every way of a man is right in his own eyes, but the Lord weighs the HEART"—the true inner self. It's very frightening to me as a psychiatrist to realize how many of even my own choices, thoughts, emotions, and motives need God's insights. We naively think we are in total control of our lives, determining maybe 20 percent of our choices while our deceiving hearts decide the other 80 percent. The Prophet Jeremiah (17:9) called our hearts more deceitful than anything, desperately evil (capable of hurting others), and hard to comprehend.

There are two kinds of salvation in Scripture. The salvation of our souls is instantaneous and eternal, occurring the moment we trust Jesus to save us from the penalty of our sins. Paul taught us in Ephesians 1:13-14 (NIV), "When you believed, you were marked in him with a seal, the promised Holy Spirit, who is a deposit guaranteeing our inheritance until the redemption of those who are God's possession." In other words, when that moment of trust occurs, we are sealed by the Spirit of God until the day of redemption—until we get to Heaven. We cannot lose the salvation of our souls once we have trusted in God. We are sealed until we get to Heaven, no matter what.

The other kind of salvation is "working out your salvation (Philippians 2:12)," which means the continual, lifelong growth process spiritually after we have obtained the first kind of salvation. This lifelong working out type of salvation is also known as sanctification—the process of growing more sanctified or holy, and God never runs out of things to sanctify us in no matter how old we are and how holy we have become. We are never perfectly sanctified until Heaven. Spiritual sanctification is a lifelong process whereby the Holy Spirit reveals more and more healing truth.

Probably most religions of the world erroneously teach that good works enable good people to work their way into Heaven. I have heard many adults, especially those facing death, say to me, "I hope my life was good enough to go to Heaven when I die." Well, the only way you could work your way into Heaven would be to live a perfect life your entire life, and only Jesus has done that so far, so I doubt you will be the first. None of us is "good enough" to win a free pass. But there is a free pass—simply putting our faith in what Jesus did on the cross to pay for our sins.

Saying "yes" to Jesus when he offers to pay for our sins makes salvation a free gift by grace (unmerited favor you cannot work to get) through simple faith. If it was from good works, we are so self-deceiving we would just become proud of our own good works and that sinful and prideful attitude would keep us out. "Not of works, lest any man should boast (Ephesians 2:8-9)." Whatever qualified the thief on the cross to go with Jesus to Heaven qualifies all.

As I grow older I am trying to be more of a human "being" rather than a human "doing." Good works are nice but only faith brings salvation. One of the best ways for believers to become sanctified, however, is daily meditation on Scripture. Bible meditation is the best way to learn the deep secrets and unconscious intents of our hearts (souls and spirits), like a sword (Hebrews 4:12). If God truly loves you and values you like silver, "He will sit as a ... purifier of silver (Malachi 3:3)." Truth that burns removes our dross.

When we see our lives as eternal, with brief pains on earth as momentary growth experiences, we can "be anxious for nothing (Ephesians 4: 6-7)." Paul said in I Corinthians 10:13 that even though God never tempts us to sin, he always shows us a way to escape if we open the eyes of our heart.

Sanctification often requires the confrontation of family and friends to point out flaws that we may not even be aware of. A superficial friend only tells you what you want to hear. A true friend will risk your anger or even rejection to confront you when needed. Loving constructive criticism often hurts first. Wise King Solomon said 3,000 years ago, "Faithful are the wounds of a friend (Proverbs 27:6)." As believers we all still sin, but hopefully not as often. We aren't perfect, just forgiven. There are 365 sins listed in the Bible and all hurt someone, and since I hate hurting others, I would try to avoid sin even if God didn't even exist. But because I am a mere human I sin every day whether by act, lack of appropriate act, thought, desire, or conscious or unconscious motives.

God has specific plans to help you grow up spiritually and become more sanctified. Dr. Tony Evans teaches, "God will often not show you what he plans to do until you do what he's asked you to do. That's called faith." Deciding to fall back into a sinful lifestyle after becoming a believer is called "worldliness," and Dr. Tony Evans also wisely but simply states, "Worldliness is rebellion against kingdomness." As a believer, I am now a citizen of the Kingdom of God and strive to live by the morals and principles of that Kingdom.

If we are willing to give God the "lemons" that fall painfully on our heads in life, he will empower us to make delicious lemonade and mature. C.S. Lewis taught us so wisely, "Try to exclude the possibility of suffering and you find that you have excluded life itself." Lewis also taught us, "Your real, new self will not come as long as you are looking for it. It will come when you are looking for him."

"No man knows how bad he is till he has tried very hard to be good."
—C.S. Lewis

Luke, a physician, said in Luke 13:34 that Jesus cried out, "O Jerusalem, Jerusalem, which killest the prophets, and stonest them that are sent unto thee; how often would I have gathered thy children together, as a hen *doth gather* her brood under *her* wings, and ye would not!" Jesus did many miracles in Jerusalem, even restoring withered limbs and raising the dead. It was obvious he was the God-Man. And Jesus called people throughout Jerusalem to put their faith in him for salvation, but very few did. Most rejected him instead of accepting his call and the call of the Holy Spirit for salvation. Jesus was so grieved over their rejection that he wept, smote his breasts, and tore his garments, crying out how he would stretch out his "wings" to save the lives of his children there—the citizens of Jerusalem—even at the expense of his own life.

Farmers know that in a hailstorm, a mother hen will spread out her wings for her little chicks to run under to save their lives. The hail will fall on the head of the mother hen and kill her, but the lives of her little chicks will be spared. This is the illustration Jesus used to show his love for the lost and his willingness to die on the cross for their salvation, like a mother hen gathers her baby chicks at her own expense.

Some believers think we have a God who creates humans that God actually wants to go to Hell. But as a psychiatrist, I imagine Jesus, wanting the people of Jerusalem to become believers but weeping over their rejection. If he created them to go to Hell, why would he weep when they rejected him, smiting his breasts. He would be schizophrenic. He gave all humans who reach an age of accountability a free will to accept or reject him and empowers them to do so if they accept him. Peter said, "The Lord is not slack concerning his promise, as some men count slackness; but is longsuffering to us-ward, not willing that any should perish, but that all should come to repentance (II Peter 3:9)."

Because we have human natures, none of us would seek a relationship with him without the call of the Holy Spirit. But those who reach an age of accountability have received the call and enablement of the Holy Spirit to turn to God for salvation and have either accepted or rejected him. If you are one of them, please accept him now. Take a break from reading this book and accept him right this very moment. The Holy Spirit is calling you to come to Jesus right this moment or you would not be reading this book. God is craving for you and all other humans to come to repentance.

From my own study of Scripture, I personally believe that every young child or baby who dies (or who dies in the womb) will go straight to Heaven. Some believe these babies and young children grow up in Heaven, while others, including myself, guess that they instantly become adults who are welcomed into Heaven. I believe every severely mentally handicapped person who never reaches an age of accountability will also go straight to Heaven when he or she dies, having a perfectly normal body and brain. Our new bodies will all be perfect like Jesus's body was after his resurrection.

There comes a time in our lives when we become mature enough in God's eyes to make a choice between seeking God and rejecting God. At that point, we have reached an "age of accountability" that is a different physical age for each human. The only people who won't be saved are those who have reached their personal age of accountability in the eyes of God, who have received the loving call of the Holy Spirit for salvation, and who have rejected that call of the Holy Spirit.

And there are degrees of Hell. For example, Jesus performed many of his miracles in Chorazin and Bethsaida, and yet they rejected his offers of salvation, so they will suffer more in Hell than people who rejected God in cities like Tyre and Sidon that did not witness the miracles of Jesus. In Matthew 11:21-22, Jesus said, "Woe to you, Chorazin! Woe to you, Bethsaida! For if the miracles had occurred in Tyre and Sidon which occurred in you, they would have repented long ago in sackcloth and ashes. Nevertheless I say to you, it will be more tolerable for Tyre and Sidon in the day of judgment than for you."

I personally believe life begins at conception and that we do not have the right to take the life of any human being. The exceptions to this would be in self-defense, in defending our country in war, for proper executions (a life for a life), and to save the life of the mother if the unborn baby is causing the definite death of the mother, which would also be self-defense in my opinion.

I believe all aborted or miscarried babies go straight to Heaven. When King David's baby died shortly after birth, David rejoiced that the baby was now in Heaven. David said he could not bring the baby back to earth, but that he (David) would be able to join the baby (in Heaven) someday. Solomon implied in Ecclesiastes chapter 4 that babies who die in the womb are actually fortunate, because they get to go to Heaven without all the hassles of earth first. So I believe abortion is wrong, but our Loving God gives special blessings and eternal salvation to aborted babies.

Aborted babies are some of the sheep many are not aware of. In some of the nations of Africa, half of all children die by the age of five. They have obviously not reached an age of accountability. So in those countries, more than half of the population will end up in Heaven—more sheep many are not aware of.

Who are God's True Sheep?

"And other sheep I have, which are not of this fold: them also I must bring, and they shall hear my voice; and there shall be one fold, *and* one shepherd (John 10:16)." I am not sure what this passage means, but I believe it includes those I have listed above. Who else it may include only God knows.

"I am the way, the truth, and the life. No one can come to the Father except through me (John 14:6)." What does this verse mean? This verse definitely implies that the only way to Heaven is by the blood of Jesus being applied to pay for our sins, which happens when we have faith in God or sincerely pray some time in our lives for God to forgive our sins. Some think that a person is only saved if he knows the story of Jesus and calls on the name of Jesus. Others think only Jesus saves us, but the person doesn't need to know all the facts—just to call on the Creator-God to forgive him and become part of his life. The latter are called Evangelical Universalists.

In our English speaking cultures, the Son of God is known as Jesus. He is known by other names in other cultures, such as "Yeshua" in Hebrew speaking cultures. So for sure one does not need to call him by his English name to be saved. Nobody ever called him Jesus when he was on earth during his public ministry.

The Bible says that God has many sheep that we don't know about. What does that mean? Nobody really knows. Some say it could even possibly mean there are intelligent beings on other planets as well as on earth, and they have to put their faith in God just like humans do. We were made in God's image but could there be other humanlike intelligent beings also created in the image of God? If so, what do they call the Son of God? I would personally guess that we are the only people created in God's emotional and spiritual image, but who am I to dogmatically say what is or is not possible in this immense universe?

To be an eternal but wise skeptic, one must not only be skeptical of things that don't have ample evidence, one must also be open to possibilities. You believe in the wind without ever actually seeing it—just the consequences of it. So we need to be open-minded enough to believe in the possibility of some things you cannot see or definitively prove. But I think it is most likely that the "other sheep" refers to people who we will be surprised to see in Heaven because we did not know God would give them eternal salvation.

The Bible tells us that even by nature around us, and the heavens above us, we can see that there is a Supreme Creator God and can put our faith in him. So how many facts about Jesus (or "Yeshua" or whatever people call Jesus in various languages) does one need to know to have enough faith to put his trust in God for salvation? We don't really know. But we know God wants us to share the gospel (the good news about Jesus) with every human on earth. This is called "the Great Commission."

So when we get to Heaven we will be surprised that there are "many sheep (believers)" that we did not know were true believers on earth. Whether they actually know the facts about Jesus dying on a cross in Jerusalem to pay for our sins and rising from the dead, or whether they do not know these specific facts, it is still true that their sins were paid for by the shed blood of Jesus, the Son of God, the only way to be saved.

We do know that Jesus promised in Matthew 5:6, "Blessed are those who hunger and thirst for righteousness, for they will be filled." This passage gives me great reassurance that if there is anyone in the world, even in a primitive tribe, who genuinely seeks after righteousness and to know the real God, he will somehow be filled and saved by God. Whether that takes a missionary, an angel, or whatever it may take (and only God really knows how many facts that person needs to know), God promises to fill that yearning.

God does not call all of us to become a professional, full-time foreign missionary. I am in awe of those who have accepted this calling. I have personally traveled to every continent of the earth, and even some difficult countries to get into, like Cuba, to train missionaries and many others to do counseling and use these helping skills to bring people to Christ. But whether in a foreign land or talking to a waiter at a local restaurant, I want to do what my mother urged me to do—as I am going about my day-by-day activities, always be on the lookout to dance with the world and spread the love of God.

The Great Commission

In Matthew 28:18-20, Jesus taught us, "All authority in heaven and on earth has been given to me. Therefore go and make disciples of all nations, baptizing them in the name of the Father and of the Son and of the Holy Spirit, and teaching them to obey everything I have commanded you. And surely I am with you always, to the very end of the age (NIV)." Jesus wants us to share the good news about Jesus to everyone in the world, but this passage is much more clear in the original Greek language it was written in. In the Greek, this command is in the passive imperative tense, so it is actually saying, "As you are going about in the world, spread the good news ..." God called my father to be a godly carpenter. He called my mother to work as a godly full-time homemaker. They did much during their lifetime not only to have missionaries on furlough stay at our home, but also to support missions financially and in much prayer at our family devotions every night of my life. I also witnessed both of them leading others to faith in Jesus. I believe God called me to become a Christian psychiatrist, author, radio host, and teacher. So as I was "going about in the world," I tried to "spread the good news." Several million people have trusted Christ through various Meier Clinic ministries.

The Apostle Paul, who wrote most of the New Testament Epistles, was proud of the acts and attitudes of genuine love that he saw in many of the people he personally discipled in Corinth. He praised them for the love they were showing to the rest of the world, surrounding them through the loving acts and attitudes that genuinely flowed from their hearts. So Paul gave them the highest compliment he could possibly give them: "Ye are our epistle written in our hearts, known and read of all men (II Corinthians 3:2)." In other words, you and the life you live are God's love letter to the people you come in contact with. Without saying a word, you are being a witness to those around you one way or another.

Paul went on to say in verse three, "Clearly you are a letter from Christ showing the result of our ministry among you. This 'letter' is not written with pen and ink, but with the Spirit of the living God. It is carved not on tablets of stone, but on human hearts."

So you, the reader, can be God's love letter to the world, by supporting and praying for and assisting missionaries throughout the world, and by being a missionary wherever you are in the world, "as you are going throughout the world"—dance with the world, a dance of the love of God.

CHAPTER TWENTY-ONE

Experiencing God through Christian Psychology

"Do not go where the path may lead; go where there is not a path and leave a trail."

—Ralph Waldo Emerson

When I graduated from my Duke psychiatry residency in 1975, there was no major field of Christian psychology. The concept was in its infancy. But I saw Christian psychology as having great potential for changing the world. There are millions of people in the world who will not read a Bible or listen to a pastor or missionary, but who will gladly listen to the same Christian principles shared with them by a psychologist or psychiatrist during times of crisis. And there were many valuable techniques and facts I learned from psychiatry research that would benefit Christians during their crises.

When I went to help pioneer a Christian counseling program at Dallas Theological Seminary in 1976, there were no Christian psychology textbooks to use for my courses, so I had to write books to use for them. My first two books were *Christian Childrearing and Personality Development* and *Happiness is a Choice*, and those books ended up selling about a million copies each. There was a thirst and vacuum for this new field. My desire to blaze a new trail was beginning to be fulfilled.

Christian psychology is simply the merging of practical biblical principles of life with beneficial research findings from psychological studies. The Book of Proverbs in the Old Testament is an excellent textbook of Christian psychology. In it, King Solomon wrote hundreds of wise sayings that benefit practical spiritual and psychological living. He did much of his own research and learned well from the experiences of others too, including his father, King David.

There are many psychological theories that are crazy and non-biblical, but all psychological research that reveals truth backs up Scripture, because Scripture is true. In James 5:16, James tells us that if we confess our faults with other human beings, it will result in spiritual healing. Psychological research discovered the same thing—that sharing our flaws with others in group therapy or in individual therapy or even in informal settings results in healing those emotional wounds. It is the reason Alcoholics Anonymous is so successful. Sharing other crises in our lives, including experiences of being abused, also brings about healing. A shared burden is half a burden.

An example of psychological techniques that are not found in Scripture but are still very beneficial to use by pastors or Christian counselors are Gestalt techniques. If you are helping an abuse victim, for example, you would normally get the client to talk about the abuse incidents until they get everything out in the open and experience healing by talk therapy. It may take 10 one-hour sessions or a hundred one-hour sessions, depending on the severity and other factors. But a Gestalt technique would be something like putting an empty chair in front of the client and asking the client to pretend the abuser was sitting in the chair. You would then get the client to call the imagined abuser by name and tell him how he or she feels about the abuser. Within moments of doing a Gestalt technique like this (or reading a letter the client wrote to the abuser but did not send), the emotions come out more quickly, with tears flowing. It sucks out the emotions, and the healing may take place in significantly fewer sessions than merely talking about the abuser and the abuse. This "sucking out" of repressed emotions is called "decathexis."

If there are any techniques that would somehow violate Scripture, don't use them. And there are. But this is not a textbook of Christian psychology, but rather a book about finding God more intimately outside the box. Using the many truths that have been discovered in the decades of development of Christian psychology to understand God outside the box would be a wise choice. It is one of many wise choices for doing so.

Following are some common practical examples of Christian psychology:

Spiritual and Emotional Health

The Meier Clinics are a national chain of nonprofit clinics that have about a hundred psychiatrists, psychologists, and therapists who see more than 2,000 clients a week. About 20 percent of the population inherit tendencies toward depression, bipolar disorder, ADHD, or other brain function chemical problems easily corrected with proper psych meds, but these meds must be taken lifelong for genetic deficiencies, just like people who inherit low thyroids have to take thyroid meds the rest of their lives to stay healthy and alive.

But the majority of clients who come to our clinics nationally can get well only using the principles of Christian psychology, which include good counseling and nutrition. Those who were happy all their lives and do not have a genetic predisposition toward depression but are going through a depressing crisis in their lives, or severe grief, may benefit from an antidepressant for three to six months to get them well more quickly so they won't lose work or have to drop out of school or college.

They won't need meds later if, in their counseling, they work though the emotional and spiritual conflicts that are causing their brain chemicals to drain—usually some form of anger turned inward, such as bitterness, unresolved grief, stuffing emotions, true guilt over something, or false guilt over not being as perfect as they erroneously expect themselves to be. We recommend weekly counseling as a minimum for those going through significant depression or anxiety.

If the depression is severe enough to render the person unable to function adequately at home, school, or work, or if there are death wishes, then we recommend our Day Program, where people come to become functional and productive again. If suicide is a risk, we recommend hospitalization to prevent it, followed by the Day Program. Anxiety is a fear of finding out the truth about our own thoughts, feelings, or motives, so our counselors are trained to dig out root problems so that the truth sets us free from anxiety and even from panic attacks.

Mark Twain once said, wisely, that "It's not what you eat that gives you indigestion—it's what's eating you!" How true. Digging out the truth takes away our fear of looking at it, so our anxiety and panic attacks disappear. But we often use medications to prevent painful panic attacks while the client is getting rid of them more slowly through counseling.

There are meds that get rid of anxiety within four minutes and keep it away for from eight to 24 hours so we can get rid of panic attacks the same day we see you, within minutes actually, if we give you meds that work right away. But there are better meds to take over the long haul that may take longer to build up. If you have bipolar disorder, or have a first-degree relative with bipolar disorder, even if you do not have it yourself, the antidepressants will not work for you probably unless you take a mood stabilizer with it, like Lamictal or Topamax, or a major tranquilizer.

Some of our meds are weight neutral, some make you gain weight, and some (like Topamax, Geodon, and stimulants, especially Vyvanse) tend to make you lose weight. So in your choice of meds, be sure to let your psychiatrist know if you prefer staying the same weight, gaining, or losing, because there are equally effective meds that can affect that either way.

For any human to have lingering happiness, peace, and meaning in life, he has to get out of the stupid human rat race—seven billion people who feel like a nobody and go through life trying to prove they are not a nobody through sex, power, money, and "fame" (even if only on Facebook!). Instead they need to learn to love and be loved by people who know all their secrets and love them anyway, and also be loved by themselves, and develop a healthy relationship with the One who created them in the first place. The Great Commandment is to love God, your neighbor, and yourself in healthy ways, and this, along with forgiving but protecting yourself from the jerks of this world, will bring you a life of love, joy, peace, good sleep, and meaning, if you also take care of the medical and other factors.

No Toxic Shame Needed: Your sins are your sins and my sins are my sins, but the good news is that God casts "all our sins into the depths of the sea (Micah 7:19)." There is therefore now "no condemnation ... (Romans 8:1)." The Apostle Paul taught us that eternal salvation is totally by grace—not by good works or it couldn't be called God's gift (Ephesians 2:8-9). Since suicide is an obvious sin, and salvation is a free gift with no good or sinful deeds involved, suicide can't lose anyone's salvation.

Some denominations may tell people they will lose their salvation if they commit suicide, in order to make them too afraid to do so. I want to do whatever I can to prevent suicide, being a psychiatrist, but I won't scare people out of it with lies. Think of the millions of loved ones who have been relatives or friends of suicide victims and now think their deceased friends or relatives are suffering in Hell when they actually aren't. Suicide is a serious sin though, and some people are being very selfish when they commit suicide to get vengeance on others or for other wrong motives. But many people commit suicide because their brain chemicals are so depleted that they have severe emotional pain and think the pain will never go away. They don't realize that they could be over their suicidal depression with a few weeks of treatment in a day program, or a longer period of time in outpatient therapy. They don't realize how much of the pain they can eliminate by merely taking an antidepressant, which helps restore their "happy brain chemicals" back to a normal level. "Assisted suicide" is a very evil and stupid practice, because anyone with suicidal depression can get over it with the right kind of help. I consider assisted suicide to be a form of murder.

Toxic shame is primarily false guilt, either for sins already forgiven or often for not living up to unrealistic expectations of parents growing up or unrealistic expectations of significant others now. When my thoughts stray, I remember this: "May the words of my mouth and the meditation of my heart be pleasing to you, O Lord (Psalm 19:14)." When callers (to live radio shows) call in to admit a sin, I often tell them my latest sin too, to illustrate that God wants us to learn from our sins, not to condemn ourselves for being human. We all sin "and fall short of the glory of God." But we are also "justified freely by his grace (Romans 3:23-24)."

So we should admit our sins and learn from them. Beating ourselves up over and over for any past sins is a worse sin, insulting the God who already covered all our sinfulness with his blood. Not accepting God's total forgiveness is playing God and punishing God's child—you—causing false guilt and toxic shame, making future sins more likely.

False guilt (shame) is one of the two main causes of nearly all addictions, the other cause being lack of connectedness with one or more people who know all your secrets and love you anyway—people you can share feelings with. When you feel guilty after genuine confession, it is not conviction, but condemnation from Satan, the "accuser of the brethren (Revelation 12:10)." It's his job!

He likes to pretend like he is God, convicting you for things that are already forgiven or even things that were never even wrong in the first place. He and his demons have studied your behavior and your family's behavior for generations back by now, and they know what guilt trips got laid on you by your parents, often accidently. So now it is easy for them to play God and lay the same false guilt trips on you to carry out their role as "accusers of the brethren."

I love C.S. Lewis's *The Screwtape Letters* book, where Satan assigns various demons to various people. If Satan assigns a couple of demons per person to falsely accuse them, then he might not assign any to you if you already beat yourself up so much you don't need any additional help from demons.

You are already a demon to yourself—a terrorist to yourself living inside your very own brain. Kick the terrorists out and become your own best friend. Make a pledge right this very moment and write it down in your Bible and date it: "From this day forward I promise to be my own best friend, and to make an attempt to quit saying anything to myself that I would not say to my best friend under the same circumstances."

This one act could very well increase your quality of life significantly, especially if you tend to think God is like your shaming, critical parent. Even the Apostle Paul sometimes did things he shouldn't and didn't do what he should (Romans 7-8), but said, "There is no condemnation." Beating yourself up for any past confessed sins is doing the work of Satan, and he already has plenty of helpers, so quit assisting him!

Trials in this Life

"A joyful countenance has nothing to do with your circumstances. Joy is a choice."

—Chuck Swindoll

"We usually can't do much to change our lot … only our reaction to our lot."

—Chuck Swindoll

"Do not wrinkle your soul with worry."

—Jack Graham

Life is what happens while we are busy making other plans. If you expect nothing you will never be disappointed! The higher your expectations of only good things happening around you in your life, the more disappointed you will be when they don't. Thousands of years ago, Job suffered horrible skin disease and loss of his children. While grieving these losses, he additionally had a nagging wife and condemning friends who insisted it must be because of his sins, even though it clearly was not. God told Job to ignore their bad advice. Job told his wife (Job 2:10), "What? Shall we expect good in life and not also expect adversity?"

I am not saying you should go through life with a negativistic attitude expecting life to be a miserable existence with little or no pleasure. God sent his son, Jesus, to earth so that we might have life, and have it more abundantly (John 10:10). But be realistic, realizing that every life has difficulties and setbacks and even tragedies if you live long enough.

Trials in life produce the normal stages of grief, which are different than depression. First you can't believe the tragic event is true. When reality hits you, you are likely to initially feel quite angry, whether you are aware of the anger or not. The anger starts out as anger toward whatever human you blame, whether accurate or not. But then the third thing that happens in almost every case of grief, but often unconsciously or subconsciously, is anger toward God—for allowing the tragic event to occur. When resolved, this is followed by genuine weeping and grief, and then resolution.

I have even, I am embarrassed to say, gotten angry at God for little negative events, like having a flat tire at an inopportune time. But what about the death of a child, the rejection of a mate, or an incident of sexual abuse? Those are severe. We not only get angry at God for allowing the cause of our grief, we often think God caused the event on purpose. God is never the author of sin, so if you are grieving because someone has sinned against you, whether by rejection or from taking advantage of you financially or for whatever reason, remember God did not cause it because he is never the author of sin. But it is still easy to get angry at God for allowing it to happen when he could very well have prevented it.

God, for some reason, lets the rain fall on the just and the unjust (Matthew 5:45), and allows bad things to happen to good people. Whenever my patients ask me why God lets them suffer, I have to admit to them that I don't really know why. If I were God, I would block every bad thing from happening to innocent victims because I love them. And yet I trust in my heart of hearts that God loves them thousands of times more than I do. He even allowed bad things to happen to his own son, Jesus. Horrible things. Even torture and murder on the cross.

So I tell my patients that when we get to Heaven, why God allows bad things to happen to good people should be one of the first things we ask Jesus about. I am convinced that when we find out why, we will finally understand why, in the long run, it was the most loving thing he could have done. Possibly, one reason he allows bad things to happen to us might be because tragic events produce greatness within us. Abraham Lincoln suffered the tragic death of his wife and other great losses, many other tragedies, and even financial bankruptcy all as stepping stones to become our greatest president.

If we never say anything negative to ourselves that we would not tell our best friend under the same circumstances, truth brings joy. What would you tell yourself if you locked your keys in your car? Would you automatically say, "You stupid idiot"? Would you say negative things to yourself for making such a simple mistake? What would you tell your best friend or mate if he or she locked her keys in the car? If you love that person, you would never say, "You stupid idiot"—unless you are a severely narcissistic jerk. You would probably say something like, "Don't feel bad. We all make mistakes. We will just get some help, and life will go on."

In other words, you would tell your close friend the truth, because that is the truth. But you would tell yourself a negative lie. Life is tough enough without living with a nagging terrorist in your brain beating you up whenever you make a mistake. People who do that have often had a nagging terrorist as a parent who frequently criticized or punished them for honest mistakes like spilling the milk as a child or forgetting to do a chore.

As a child, you believe the authority figures in your life operate on truth, which they often do not! You come to believe you are a particularly flawed human being who deserves the wrath not only of those authority figures but also of yourself.

Many people decide what sins they want to commit, and then find a religion that will back them up. But all sins are depressing in the long run, even though they are fun for a short season. Overly emotional people are especially prone toward sexual sins. Evangelists are a vital part of God's plan, but evangelists have a many times greater rate of having affairs than even atheistic psychiatrists do with their clients. This leads to depression not only in the ones having the affairs but also in the families who suffer the horrible results of these affairs.

Bitterness

The Apostle Paul advises us, "Look after each other so no poisonous root of bitterness grows up to trouble you, corrupting many (Hebrews 12:15)." Bitterness is the number one cause of death. It causes a host of unhealthy biochemical changes in our minds and bodies, resulting in fewer antibodies. This makes us more likely to come down with infections and other diseases. Bitterness also depletes some of the serotonin out of our brains, causing depression. Bitterness is a foolish decision. Bitterness is like swallowing rat poison and hoping it hurts the other guy.

Unconscious Sins

When we sin on purpose, those are called "conscious sins." But almost everything we do is influenced by our unconscious thoughts, feelings, and motives. Therefore, we often commit "unconscious sins"—sins that we do not even realize are sins. James so aptly gifts us with the insight that we see life through darkly dimmed glass and walk away from life's mirror with a tainted memory. All sins hurt somebody, but we can be easily tricked into committing unconscious sins, so "be on guard—be courageous—be strong, and do everything with love (I Corinthians 16:13-14)." Good people don't want to hurt others by sinning, but we are often blind to our own unconscious sins. We can submit ourselves to God, who says "Resist the devil, and he will flee from you (James 4:7)."

Around 1000 BC, night travel was by foot, with an ankle lamp, so "Thy word is a lamp to guide my feet and a light for my path (Psalm 119:105)." Meditating on God's word soaks into our brains and helps us the rest of our lives by remaining a light for our path in life. As a psychiatrist I often hear "to enjoy today" as the goal in life for many young people in particular, but "the prudent understand where they are going (Proverbs 14:8)."

The wise have a goal in life more significant than to just enjoy today. The most idiotic thing I do here on planet earth is to occasionally get angry at God for convicting me of sins (called "folly" in Proverbs 19). Solomon said, "A person's folly subverts his way and his heart rages against the Lord (Proverbs 19:3)." We use denial to lie to ourselves to justify sin then get mad at God for revealing our sins to us. But hopefully we then agree with God and grow.

Conflict Resolution

Wise King Solomon said in Proverbs 14:29: "The one who is slow to anger has great understanding," In every argument, pause long enough to imagine that your soul is stepping outside your body to observe the argument and analyze it. Then do whatever your more objective soul says to do to handle that particular argument. I have tried this not only myself, but on clients for many years, and it works well.

Some relationships improve with tactful confrontation. Others get worse. Solomon advised in Proverbs 9:8, "Do not reprove a mocker or he will hate you." In Proverbs 9:8, Solomon also says that if you reprove a wise person (not a fool), he'll love you more.

Growing Stronger from Tragedies

"Be thankful in all circumstances (I Thessalonians 5:18)" seems humanly impossible and totally illogical—unless your life goal is spiritual maturity. Being thankful in all circumstances doesn't mean not getting angry, ashamed, or grief-stricken first. When someone is grieving a loss, we're to weep with those who weep. I've had some varied, horrible losses in my life that I humanly wish had never occurred, but what's the value of the insights I have gained? Here's a research experiment for you to try. Ask several wise people you know who are 60 years old or older what events in their lives produced their greatest growth. My prediction is that it will nearly always be after their greatest losses.

There are Solutions for Every Problem

I sometimes feel like I am in one "impossible situation" after another, but then I think, "How many solutions could Jesus think of? He is God. He could think of hundreds of possible solutions to this seemingly impossible situation. I just need for Jesus to show me one of them!" Then I can pray with confidence.

Value of Discipline

Dr. James Dobson's grandson, when asked what changed when he got disciplined earlier that morning, replied seriously, "I got a new attitude!"

Addictions or Failures in Our Lives

Proverbs 26:11 tells us that foolish people keep going back to the same failures just like dogs go back to their own vomit and lick it up again. A dog will eat rotten food, vomit it up, walk away, then turn around and come back to his vomit thinking "Ah, a warm meal!"

What's sad is that all of us are foolish at times, failing in the same ways over and over like a foolish dog returning to his own vomit. God understands our temptations to fail, teaching us in Proverbs that if someone fails seven times but keeps trying, he's a righteous man! Even the Apostle Paul said in Matthew 7-8 that he sometimes fails to do what he should, and also fails by doing what he shouldn't, but God forgives. Paul taught us in Romans 8:1 that when we do fail, "There is now therefore no condemnation." God wants us to learn and grow from our failures.

Men versus Women

Big boys don't cry, we are taught growing up. But men die younger than women. I believe that is primarily because men tend to repress their emotions, and repressed anger is the leading cause of death. Depression, as we stated, is anger turned inward. Men apparently attempt suicide less often but succeed much more often than women, probably because their choice of suicide is more likely to be a gun to the head or hanging, whereas women often survive overdose attempts or cutting of the wrists. Research shows that single men in America have 300 percent more heart attacks, strokes, and suicides than married men. Marriage makes only a 2 percent difference in women! "He that finds a wife finds a good thing, and obtains favor of the Lord (Proverbs

18:22)." The Bible never says "She who finds a husband finds a good thing!" The right man can bring companionship and lifelong romance to a woman, and the right woman can to a man. But wives help us men to feel, and I think that is why we gain more than they do from male/female relationships!

Studies have clearly shown that husbands and wives who have a deeper relationship with God will often pray together, some daily, and couples who do so have a much better sex life than couples who do not. So you men who are reading this book, if you want a good sex life, you are more likely to have one the closer you and your mate get to the real God. This book, hopefully, will benefit you even in surprising ways like that. A good sex life is good for women too. It releases endorphins that not only draw you and your mate closer together in an emotionally binding relationship, but these endorphins also improve your happiness level and quality of life. These are good parting thoughts from Christian psychology that will benefit your relationship with God and with each other.

CHAPTER TWENTY-TWO

The Christian Psychology
Movement in Other Nations

├─────────────────────────────────┤

T he Christian psychology movement is growing and helping people around the world but is strongest in the United States. Over my lifetime, I have had the wonderful opportunity to meet and minister to thousands of people in many countries around the world, including every continent. But the purpose of this book is not a history of the growth of the Christian psychology movement, but rather how the Christian psychology movement can assist you in drawing closer to the real and true Creator-God outside the box. In this chapter, I would like to share just two true stories of how God intervened to help spread the movement in Sweden and in Russia. I choose these two stories because they really show how the God outside the box moves and directs and shows up behind the scenes.

The Christian Psychology Movement in Sweden

In 1992, I got a phone call from a Lutheran minister in Sweden, Rev. Dan Rosendahl. He told me his wife, Joyce, was near death and needed help and wanted my advice on what could be done. Their five children were all very heartbroken about their mother's condition as well. She had become so depressed and anxious that her brain became swollen—a very rare condition. The doctors in Sweden had tried steroids and other treatments, but nothing worked and their family doctor told them to prepare for Joyce to die if the condition did not improve.

I told Dan and Joyce to come to Dallas, Texas, where I would treat her daily at our Day Program. When I got to know Joyce and her life history, I discovered that what was really eating away at her were flashbacks of severe abuse she had suffered during her childhood. Our staff dug and probed for six weeks before Joyce came to a complete recovery and was filled with joy to replace the depression and severe anxiety with peace.

When Joyce got back to her doctors in Sweden, they and the people who knew her were all amazed at her "miracle recovery in Dallas," and articles were even written about her recovery in the newspapers around Sweden. As a result, Joyce and Dan Rosendahl decided to dedicate their lives to spreading Christian psychology throughout Sweden the best they could. There was no such thing as "Christian psychology" in Sweden in 1992 for all practical purposes. By early 1993, I flew to Sweden at my own expense to teach a large group of psychiatrists, psychologists, therapists, and pastors for an entire week on various aspects of Christian psychology.

Very few of the mental health professionals were Christians, but by the end of the week, more than half of them had trusted Jesus for salvation and were ready to become Christian therapists who would integrate the Bible into their therapy. One was a female psychiatrist, who decided to give a large portion of her income to promote the Christian psychology movement in Sweden, offering support for Joyce and Dan to spend a great deal of their time spreading the good news. And they did. They got opportunities to talk all over the country about what Joyce had learned during her Day Program therapy in Dallas.

Swedish government officials even asked Dan and Joyce to consult them on how to set up a Day Program that used the techniques we used at our Dallas clinic. They have government health care in Sweden, and people who request that kind of treatment can receive it now in Sweden.

I stayed in touch with Dan and Joyce over the years, and other therapists from various Meier Clinics went to Sweden for seminars, including our child psychiatrist Dr. Paul Warren (now deceased). In 2010, however, I received a sad phone call from Joyce and Dan. Joyce had developed incurable leukemia, which had not responded to two separate chemotherapy treatment programs. During the final few weeks of her life, I was on the phone with Joyce and Dan numerous times to comfort them and prepare them and their children for her death.

After Joyce died, Dan Rosendahl compiled an email to send to all their loved ones, including me. In the email, Dan wrote: "During this last period of four weeks Joyce encouraged us all to talk about what we experienced and to cry and laugh as we felt the need to do so. She shared so many sound attitudes and advice with her entire family that she was both grieving and rejoicing while she was in the process of dying. The advice she got from Dr. Meier to let other people love her she embraced wholeheartedly and her spirit was lifted as she felt loved from all who came to say farewell. Joyce and I were in frequent contact with Dr. Meier during the last month of her life, which he says ministered to him even more than he was ministering to comfort and prepare us for her death. On her tombstone she wanted the word 'Loved' to be written. It is being made as I write this. It will be made of black granite with gold letters and the 'Resurrection Cross' on the side."

The Christian Psychology Movement in Russia

After President Yeltsin took over Russia, Christianity was allowed in Russia, and God provided an open door for me to come and teach Christian psychology for two weeks in Moscow and St. Petersburg. I was excited to be able to stand in Red Square in Moscow, toasting Yeltsin's soldiers with a Coca Cola in my hand for their successful takeover of the former Communist regime.

In Moscow, I met with psychiatrists, psychologists, and therapists to have informal discussions of Christian psychology. But in St. Petersburg, I actually got to teach a large class of future school psychologists for an entire week at St. Petersburg University (formerly Leningrad University). There were more than 100 students. When I shared with them case study after case study, they were often in tears as they heard about the recoveries. I taught, of course, through an interpreter. By the end of the week, God had really moved in their lives. They were nearly all atheists, but half of them trusted Christ by the end of the week after I got them to weep about their losses and their parents and being totally dominated by their former government. They said they intended to practice Christian psychology with the students they would counsel someday in the high schools of Russia. There were many extraordinary events that took place during that week that I will not go into in this book, but I will relate a few, like the day my ride to go teach did not show up, and I was afraid I was going to miss teaching that day. A complete stranger pulled up and asked me what was wrong as I stood, obviously frustrated, on the street corner, and he drove me straight to the class just in time. But perhaps the most interesting and miraculous experience was when I went to speak to whoever showed up at a meeting of psychologists who might want to hear the kind of therapy I did at the Meier Clinics in America. Only one psychologist showed up, an atheist, and I was initially very disappointed. But I would love to tell you her miraculous true story.

Case Study: Atheist Psychologist in Russia

One night my friend and I hired a 20-year-old Russian student we had never met before to be our interpreter, since I know only a few words of Russian. We met with a 55-year-old female Russian psychologist. She was the only one who showed up to the meeting that we had invited some psychologists to. I gave her a copy of the Bible in Russian, and she angrily threw it to the seat next to hers, telling me through our interpreter that she wanted to hear about my psychiatric techniques in America, which she had heard about, but not anything about God, "since there isn't any," she insisted.

She was obviously very angry at "God," like so many atheists are. In the back of my mind, I was guessing that she probably was very lonely and depressed and angry, and that she probably had an absent father, and thus probably married an "absent" male to fill the father vacuum in her heart, but it was obvious her love tank had never been filled. So I made a proposal to her.

"Dr. Lansky, rather than tell you about my techniques, can I pretend for a few minutes like you are a new patient of mine, and I will pretend like I am doing therapy on you. Then you will really see what I do."

She said, "Yes, Dr. Meier, I would really like to learn what you do in that way."

"Well, Dr. Lansky, was your father gone too much when you were growing up?" I asked. I could immediately see a tear forming in Dr. Lansky's eye. She was quite shocked at my question.

"Well, yes, Dr. Meier. He was a sailor, and he was nice to us when he was home, but he was home only three days every six months."

"How old were you when he died?"

"Seventeen." She began weeping quietly, trying to hold in her pain.

Showing warmth and compassion, I then told her through our interpreter, "When your father died, that must have been an enormous loss for you, because your fantasy also died that day."

"What fantasy, Dr. Meier?"

"The fantasy that your father would someday retire and spend lots of time with you and show you the love of a father that you needed so much."

At this she wept loudly and profusely, nodding her head yes.

"Dr. Lansky, did you then marry someone distant like your father out of a codependent need to 'fix' your father by trying fruitlessly to 'fix' a distant husband, because that is what most young women with your childhood background would have done."

Astounded, she replied, "Yes, Dr. Meier, and we just divorced finally last year when I gave up on ever changing him." She wept even louder, then stopped long enough to ask me, "How did you know all these things about me?"

"I was just guessing," I replied, which is the truth, except I think God was helping me because I was praying the whole time that he would, but I couldn't tell her that because I promised her I wouldn't mention God to her when she got angry at the beginning.

I got her to forgive her father for dying on her and her husband for being just like her father. We used Gestalt techniques, where she pretended to talk to each of them sitting in an empty chair. After doing that, she was ready to ask me about God on her own. And after a pause, she did ask my friend and I a question about God. I don't even remember now what the question was, but my friend from Campus Crusade then began to answer her question by quoting a Bible passage. I remembered memorizing those verses myself not too long before that.

But then my friend couldn't remember the second half of the passage and he looked at me, and I couldn't remember either, and I told my friend that I couldn't remember where that passage was found either, and neither could he. We were momentarily frustrated, but then what I think was a genuine miracle of God occurred.

Sache, the 20-year-old interpreter we had just hired, reached over and grabbed the Russian Bible that Dr. Lansky had thrown down beside her, opening it without turning any pages, and finished reading the exact passage to her. Then he got very scared, realizing what he had just done, and dropped the Bible and explained first to Dr. Lansky in Russian, then to us in English, what he had just done. He knew nothing about that passage before.

Dr. Lansky sobbed with happier tears now, realizing that she had just experienced something that almost had to be supernatural. The interpreter turned to me and my friend, crying and shocked himself, asking, "How was I able to do that just now?" I replied, "Sache, God enabled you to do that because he loves Dr. Lansky, and he loves you too."

Dr. Lansky, upon hearing that statement translated into Russian, replied back to me, "Not only is there a God, but he made himself known to me tonight."

"And to me too," Sache, the interpreter, added.

(CHAPTER TWENTY-THREE)

Experiencing God through Dreams

There are more than 150 verses in the Bible about how God uses dreams and speaks to us in the "night seasons." But one of my favorites is from Job, who suffered greatly—even without any personal sin involved—for God's glory. Job said:

"For God speaks again and again, though people do not recognize it. He speaks in dreams, in visions of the night, when deep sleep falls on people as they lie in their beds. He whispers in their ears and terrifies them with warnings. He makes them turn from doing wrong; he keeps them from pride. He protects them from the grave, from crossing over the river of death … listen to me. Keep silent and I will teach you wisdom (Job 33:14-18, 33:33, New Living Translation)."

Dreams are windows into our souls. We nearly all dream four or five times a night, but only remember them when we happen to awake during one of them. A female patient of mine dreamed that her husband was driving their car with her riding in the backseat. Can you guess what their problem was? Dreams are "movies" that our unconscious writes and directs. We often play more than one character, sometimes even an animal with emotions.

Now as a psychiatrist, I feel compelled to warn you about dreams. Don't put too much stock in them, but don't ignore them either. The Bible contains scores and scores of examples of how God led many of his children through dreams, like Mary, Joseph, Jacob, Daniel, and many others. In fact, King David wrote to us in Psalm 16:7 that God teaches our hearts in our dreams.

So let me ask you a question. If you were single and had a dream tonight in which you married a certain person whom you know, then had another intense dream the same night in which God was urging you to move to Alaska, how would you interpret those dreams. Is God telling you in those dreams that he wants you to marry that person and move to Alaska? It is possible, but probably not. And if you are already married to someone else (or the person you dreamed about is) and you don't both have biblical grounds for divorce (Matthew 5, Matthew 19, and I Corinthians 7), then you can know for certain that God is never going to call you to disobey Scripture in a dream or any other way.

In fact, it is possible that God is telling you that it would be better for you to move to Alaska rather than to marry that jerk! Or God may be telling you something else. Or he may not be telling you anything in those two dreams, except for you to pray about them briefly to see if there is something you can learn from the dreams that will help you become more like Jesus.

I have asked many hundreds of clients about their dreams, and have seen common themes and patterns in those dreams in relationship with their circumstances. Violent dreams usually imply buried anger toward others if others are getting hurt in the dreams. If my client is getting chased or hurt, that usually implies past hurts or a fear of getting hurt by someone. Our dreams reveal truth but also disguise it to make it easier to bear, so animals may represent yourself or others in the dream.

If you are caring for a young child in the dream, you may be the adult and the child, with the child representing a time in your life when you, as an adult, need to take care of and heal the wounded child within you. Falling dreams usually represent times in your life when you feel like you are failing at something. Flying dreams are usually good dreams, representing times in your life when you feel like you are growing emotionally or spiritually or are succeeding at something. If you dream you are traveling in a car but are in the backseat while your mate is driving, that implies that your mate be overly controlling you, or that you may be overly dependent and wanting your mate to "drive your life."

Throughout this book, I have shared my own significant dreams through which God clearly directed my life in specific directions. For more information on dreams, I co-authored an entire book on dream interpretation called *Windows of the Soul* (Thomas Nelson, Publisher).

Actual Case Study

Kaley was a 27-year-old female professional woman who came to my Day Hospital for treatment of seven straight years of suicidal depression that got worse every July. We dug and probed, looking for a root cause. Kaley had a normal family and no genetic history of depression. Kaley also denied having done anything in July seven years earlier, when it began, or of experiencing any traumatic event that might be causing her to have repressed bitterness or guilt. Depression is usually anger-turned-inward, which depletes serotonin from our brains, the chemical needed for love, joy, peace, patience, and good sleep. The anger can be toward God, others, or even yourself, in the form of guilt or shame.

After a frustrating week of not turning up her root problem, which my team rarely has trouble doing, I asked Kaley if I could pray with her in my office. She was a Christian and seemed to appreciate it. I felt led to pray that God would give her a dream that night, giving her insight into her root problem.

I asked Kaley the next day if she had a dream, and she was disappointed that she hadn't, but I told her the dream I had about her that night. In my dream, Jesus told me to ask her about an abortion. I ask every patient during my workup whether they had any miscarriages or abortions so we can do the necessary therapy to bring healing, and she had adamantly denied ever having one during my initial evaluation of her. But when I told her about my dream about her having had an abortion, Kaley admitted that she had lied to me about not having one, that she was pro-abortion, and that it hadn't bothered her to get one.

When I asked her when she got it, she paused to figure it out and it had been in July, seven years earlier, precisely when her depression began. "That has to be a coincidence," she insisted. So I said that we shouldn't assume that it was or wasn't related to the abortion, but asked her to do a homework assignment to find out. "No problem," she told me.

So I asked Kaley to guess if the aborted baby was a boy or girl, give it the name she might have used, and assume the baby was happily in Heaven with God (based on David's baby who died at birth, with David saying he would be able to join the baby someday, and on Ecclesiastes 4, which indicates that babies who die in the womb join God). I asked her to write a letter to her child in Heaven, sharing her honest emotions with her child, including looking forward to joining the child in Heaven someday. "No problem," she insisted again.

But that night, when Kaley wrote the letter, a Gestalt technique, it sucked out her repressed emotions, and she spent most of the next three days weeping, grieving, confessing, and asking for God's forgiveness, all with no prompting to do so by us—we didn't need to. Then she recovered from her seven-year depression and went on with her life, but with a more intimate relationship with God.

Case Study #2: Jennifer's Story

Jennifer was a 36-year-old happily married woman who was bitterly depressed with suicidal thoughts and had no idea why. Neither did we, in spite of digging and probing for a week in our Day Program. I asked her every day if she had any dreams the night before, and finally she did. In her dream she was a seven-year-old little girl, frozen in a large ice cube sitting on a frozen lake. I told her from her dream it seemed like something traumatic must have occurred when she was seven that "froze" her emotional growth in one way or another. But she did not remember any childhood trauma.

I asked her to call her older sister and younger sisters on the phone that night, to see if they remembered any traumatic events in their family about that time in their lives. The girls were two years apart. Both of her sisters broke down and cried and said they had never told a soul, but their maternal grandfather had sexually abused both of them. When Jennifer heard that, she was initially shocked, but then had immediate flashbacks of specific details. She remembered what her grandfather was wearing, how he smelled, and that it was while he was babysitting Jennifer at his home after grandma had died, and that it happened on the stairway to the second floor.

There is such a thing as "false memory syndrome," by which some people think they remember being sexually or otherwise abused, and it never really happened. But with false memory syndrome the memories are usually quite vague in nature. When they are as specific as Jennifer's, and are similar to the experiences of her own sisters, it is almost certainly true.

We had Jennifer place her grandfather in an empty chair and tell him how she felt about what he had done to her, and she screamed with rage and then wept profusely. After dealing with the trauma in therapy for another week, Jennifer's depression was gone and she was ready to quit the Day Program and step down to weekly individual therapy for a month or two to reinforce what she had learned and processed. Her dream was the key to finding out her root problem.

CHAPTER TWENTY-FOUR

The Problem of Bible Mistranslations

I have a seminary degree from Dallas Theological Seminary and am an ordained minister in addition to being an MD-psychiatrist. After all my studies, I wholeheartedly believe in the inerrancy of Scripture in its original languages (primarily Hebrew for the Old Testament and Greek for the New Testament), but no English versions of the original languages are perfect. They are close, but all have some errors of mistranslation. These mistranslations cause a great deal of division and pain for Christians because they mislead them into thinking some wrong teaching is God's teaching. When we get off on the wrong track, away from God's original intent, we always suffer.

Bible translators are hired from the various denominations, and pride leads some of them to "prove" their pet misbeliefs by putting in the wrong words to replace the Greek or Hebrew. Some publishers let them get away with it, in my opinion, to please them and sell more books to make more money. I have known fellow professors who are honest men who served on translation committees for new versions of the Bible. They were always true to the original languages. But others on their committees were not—fortunately only rarely—but even rare mistranslations are tragic and against the will of God, and I am sure incurs his wrath.

Throughout most of the past 2,000 years, Christians have not had entire Bibles to study for themselves. Only the priests did, so the church members had to trust the interpretations of their priests, which were often incorrect. Finally, in 1611, the King James version of the Bible made it possible for everybody to have copies of the Bible to study for themselves to see what is so and what is not so. But the King James Version was translated by spiritual leaders of The Church of England, who put their own slant on some of the passages, but translated most of the Bible quite accurately. The errors they made (I believe on purpose, personally) have hurt many Christians and kept others from becoming Christians. Some examples are in the areas of divorce and remarriage, salvation, and achieving perfection.

The English versions of Luke 16 say it is a sin to marry a divorced woman, but it never says that in the original Greek. The Greek word God put in Luke 16 is "apoluo" (married but abandoned). The Greek word for "divorce" is "apostasian," which never appears in Luke 16 at all. God does hate unnecessary divorces, and I do too, being a psychiatrist who sees the pain they cause, but it doesn't say that in Malachi 2:16. God wrote in Malachi 2:16, in the original Hebrew, that he hates abandonment, and that if you are abandoning your mate, it will hinder your prayers. God wants all of us to love and be loved, just the way we are, so if we quit abandoning our marital relationship and renew it, he'll bless us.

Satan uses mistranslations to eliminate divorced Christians from God's Army, to neglect abandonment, and to get divorced Christians to hate themselves for not being perfect. God says a pastor should be a monogamist (if married, married to one person at that time). Some of the greatest pastors I know are divorced. Christians are not supposed to take other Christians to court, for example, according to Scripture. But the Bible also says that if you have something against someone who has done you an injustice, you should confront that person first, then confront him with a witness, and even take it to the church if needed. If he still doesn't repent and correct the injustice, you should "treat him like a non-believer" and go ahead and take him to court (Matthew 18:15-17). This process is taken to eliminate as many court cases as possible between believers so they won't give Christianity a bad name.

> ¹⁵ *"If your brother sins against you, go and show him his fault, just between the two of you. If he listens to you, you have won your brother over. ¹⁶But if he will not listen, take one or two others along, so that 'every matter may be established by the testimony of two or three witnesses.' ¹⁷If he refuses to listen to them, tell it to the church; and if he refuses to listen even to the church, treat him as you would a pagan or a tax collector* (Matthew 18:15-17)."

If you attend a church that makes divorced people second-class citizens, God wants your gifts in his army, so go to a truly biblical church that won't discriminate against you erroneously. In I Corinthians 7:15-16 the Bible tells us that if you are married to an unbeliever and he or she abandons you, let them go. Divorce is permitted. In fact, it is in the passive imperative tense, so it is almost encouraged.

I personally met with and discussed this I Corinthians 7 passage with five leading pastors in America, all authors and popular in the media, and all very good men in my own personal opinion. They are men whose wisdom and integrity I trust. I asked them if the Matthew 18 court principles apply to this passage as well. In other words, if a Christian is abandoned by a Christian mate, does the abandoned Christian confront the abandoning mate one on one, then with one or two witnesses, and then with the church, and if the abandoning mate still does not repent and reconnect with the abandoned mate, can the abandoned mate then treat the mate like a nonbeliever and take him or her to divorce court?

All five pastors said they personally believe that is what the Bible is saying, but four of the five asked me not to quote them by name because their churches do not hold that view (except for the one pastor) and they get in trouble with their elder boards when they bring up their positions on this subject. As a result, there are many Christians who have been abandoned for years by their believing mates but feel stuck in a life without romantically loving and being loved, when loving and being loved again is available to them if these five pastors are correct.

Another common misconception in Christianity is that if someone becomes a Christian all their addictions and spiritual/emotional problems go away that moment, rather than the truth—that sanctification begins and the process of spiritual growth is set in motion that never gets us to perfection until we are dead and in Heaven. To be specific, in II Corinthians 5:17, the English versions of the Bible erroneously say that if anyone becomes a Christian, all things "have become new." But it never says that. God says that becoming a believer begins a lifelong process of everything (original Greek) "becoming new." "Have become new" is never there. What is sad is that people become Christians—which is great—but then are taught this misconception from the pulpit and then experience setbacks in their Christian life, as we all do, and think they must not have ever gotten saved in the first place. They feel like utter failures. Some, who are extreme perfectionists, even commit suicide.

Other perfectionists commit suicide when they read the English versions of Matthew 5:48 or II Timothy 3:17, which erroneously say to "be perfect"—and they can't. The publishers allow these errors to please the translators they hire from various denominations who teach the heresy that Christians should be perfect and sinless and have to get saved again if they do sin. In reality, the Greek words in these passages are either "artios" or "telios," both of which mean to be mature, not perfect.

The Book of Enoch

I believe in the inerrancy of Scripture in its original languages, but the Bible also favorably quotes other books like the Book of Enoch and several others. The books quoted favorably in the Bible may not be inerrant, but the Bible wouldn't quote them if they weren't worth digging for truth. If God didn't want you to read them, he wouldn't quote them. Logical?

"Those who love my holy name … I will place each of them on a throne of glory, of glory peculiarly his own (Book of Enoch 105:26)." Jude (verse 14) and other authors of the Bible quote the Book of Enoch, 7th from Adam as Jude himself says, so whether it should have been included in the Canon or not, it is definitely a book worthy of being read and studied. Enoch was a prophet and is one of only two people who went straight to Heaven without dying, the other being Elijah. I believe Enoch and Elijah might be the two witnesses who come to earth during the Great Tribulation to prophesy from Jerusalem protected by God until they are allowed to be killed and then resurrected three days later.

The Book of Enoch was either written by Enoch himself or compiled from his teachings by descendants of Noah, Enoch's great-grandson. A copy of the Book of Enoch was found in the Dead Sea Scrolls, and that particular copy was radiocarbon dated to at least 200 years BC. It discusses the trinity and many future prophetic events, some similar to the Book of Revelation written thousands of years later. That is probably why it was left out of the Old Testament by most Hebrew scholars over the centuries who did not like the triune God concept.

In the New Testament Book of Jude, verses 14-15, we read, "And Enoch also, the seventh from Adam, prophesied of these, saying, Behold, the Lord cometh with ten thousands of his saints, to execute judgment upon all, and to convince all that are ungodly among them of all their ungodly deeds which they have ungodly committed, and of all their hard speeches which ungodly sinners have spoken against him." Enoch, many thousands of years before Christ, was predicting the Second Coming of Christ the Messiah. And Jude himself said it was the actual teaching of Enoch, seventh from Adam.

Liberal scholars, of course, scoff at any such thing, as they usually do, but still have to make as their worst-case scenario that it was compiled a couple hundred years before Christ since the copy found in the Dead Sea Scrolls was radiocarbon dated to that age. That itself, with predictions of the

Second Coming and the triune God and all, would be incredible even if Jude were somehow lying about it being the actual words of Enoch.

I am not writing this to push for Christians to include Enoch in the canon as an actual book of the Bible, although it could be that it should have been included in the actual Bible. But I am writing this so that if you really want to experience God outside the box, there may be things you can learn spiritually that will draw you closer to the real God by reading some of the other books quoted in the Bible, like Enoch, my favorite extra-biblical book.

(CHAPTER TWENTY-FIVE)

Atheism

|————————————————————————————|

Our views of God are tainted by fear of rejection by peers or family, parenting styles as children, church backgrounds if any, and other environmental influences, so seek truth. Don't assume that your views of God (or of atheism) are correct. Again, search for truth. Those with no father, or an absent father, or an abusive father, are more likely to become atheists. But, in my opinion, as I've noted earlier, atheism requires more blind faith than any other God-view. All humans, even atheists, are wise to pray, "God, if you do exist, I want to discover truth about you and to personally know you." What is there to lose? Why fear doing that? I believe that if you do that, God will vote "yes." Do you remember Deuteronomy 4:29? If you seek for him with all your heart and soul, you will find him, satisfaction guaranteed. Whoever calls on him will be saved (Romans 10:13).

Billions of humans pray rote prayers daily to obey family and peers who often would kill them if they dared pray for truth and left customs. It is easy to see why those who see such absurd religious practices would be tempted to "throw out the baby with the dirty bathwater" by jumping to the false conclusion that God must not exist at all.

Terroristic religious practices by various major religions throughout human history have turned many away from God altogether, even though the true God is a God of love. I love the atheists I know personally, and I respect their right to differences of opinion, but many came from crazy legalistic religious homes. When I was in medical school, even the study of the human body convinced me that there must be a Creator-God. To think that 30 trillion cells in a human, each with thousands of enzymes, all bounced together out of nothing requires much more faith than I could ever have. As a psychiatrist I don't talk to atheists about God, but rather about father conflicts. Then they often find God naturally.

A number of biblical historical facts seem impossible to many educated people today, but with God, all things are possible. Noah's Ark seems stupid to most scientists, but what if Noah had a baby pair of wolves and all doglike species evolved "after their kind." Geneticists are saying that all species of dogs seem to have a little "wolf genes" in them. I believe Noah did this with other "kinds" of animals—not every species of animal at that time, which would be impossible. The Bible simply states that Noah's ark was loaded with different kinds of animals in pairs. I believe baby animals of each of those chosen kinds are the logical conclusion to draw, not enormous elephants, etcetera. There's no room in an ark for every species of land animal, but there was plenty of room for a baby pair of each chosen kind of land animal. Almost every major culture in the world has a worldwide flood historical record. Genetic research could be used to see the kinds Noah saved.

In Texas I waded in a shallow stream with one foot in an ancient dinosaur footprint and my other foot in an ancient human footprint beside it. Humans obsess about saving every nearly extinct species, even if it's a rat, but there are likely a million or more new species every year. Even if we all stayed in bed every day to protect rare species, we'd have to avoid killing rare species of bedbugs! There are millions of nearly extinct species, and probably a million a year that become extinct. It is necessary. It is part of survival of the fittest. We need to experience "animals outside the box" too. There are some nearly extinct species that are important to save, however. So, with all of this in mind, it should be easy to see how Noah saving dozens of baby pairs of kinds of animals could evolve into the millions of species we have today.

Before Noah's flood there was probably a vapor canopy around the world keeping the temperature on earth relatively the same all over. It would protect humans from radioactivity as well, explaining why humans in the Bible lived to such ripe old ages prior to the flood but not after the flood. With the flood, waters came down from the sky (rain plus the destruction of the vapor canopy?) and up from under the ground, so suddenly there were areas of earth that were very hot and others that were quick-frozen. Many "prehistoric" animals have been found quick frozen and buried in glaciers, many with tropical food particles also still frozen in their stomachs.

I would live the Christian life the best I could even if I were a sensible atheist, because I know it brings the most joy and satisfaction and self-worth. The fact that it does is one more proof that Christianity is the truth. I've meditated on Scripture almost daily since age ten, but I sometimes fear the painful insights promised to occur in Hebrews 4:12. There are times that the Bible gives me painful insights and I almost wish it wasn't true for selfish reasons. But these painful insights end up helping me grow up.

As I've said before, I wrote in the inside cover of my Bible at age 16, "This book will keep you from sin, but sin will keep you from this book." It's still true. The Bible is "sharper than any two-edged sword" and matures us by revealing our unconscious "thoughts and purposes of the heart (Hebrews 4:12)." In many ways this slogan is often true: The truth will set you free, but first it will make you feel miserable!

I believe that many atheists are atheists because they fear the insights they would gain from Scripture. The more truth I see within myself, the more control I have over my own life, rather than allowing my unconscious self to control me. Since sins all hurt somebody, my life's goal is to dance the dance of love by helping, not hurting, others. I want and need painful insights to sin less often.

Even if there were no God or "sins," I know from experience and psychological research that I want to look back on a life of loving, not using, my "family" of fellow human beings. It's one thing to know the laws of the land and the laws of the Bible, but "it is obeying the law that makes us right in his sight (Romans 2:13)." Mature self-love is not vanity: "The one who acquires wisdom loves himself; the one who preserves understanding will prosper (Proverbs 19:8)." The Great Commandment is to love God, self, and others. Your own "love tank" needs to be full enough to pour that love onto others. Legalists think it is godly to hate yourself, then arrogantly think they are more spiritual than those who don't! Atheists hear that kind of legalism and get turned off to Christianity, and I can't blame them.

God's awesome creativity is seen throughout the universe, from galaxies to atomic particles, but "we are God's masterpiece (Ephesians 2:10)." If you want to know if there is a God, just look in a mirror at yourself, because nobody but God could have created a being as awesome as you are. If we see ourselves in God's eyes, forgiven and loved, we can love ourselves, delight in the Lord, and dance with all around us to spread it! Paula White has said, "God's Word is the most powerful source in the world. When things try to stand in our way and prevent you—it moves them! God's Word ultimately is what has led millions of atheists to become devout believers."

Quotes to Ponder

"If you really study science, it will bring you closer to God."
—**Dr. James Tour**, Nanoscientist, Rice University

"I believe that the science of chemistry alone almost proves the existence of an intelligent creator."
—Thomas Edison

"If there were no God, there would be no atheists."
—G.K. Chesterton

"All I have seen teaches me to trust the Creator for all I have not seen."
—Ralph Waldo Emerson

"There are two ways to live: you can live as if nothing is a miracle; you can live as if everything is a miracle."
—Albert Einstein

"All men's souls are immortal, but the souls of the righteous are immortal and divine."
—Socrates

"Man will ultimately be governed by God or by tyrants."
—Benjamin Franklin

"Who buys a minute's mirth to wail a week, or sells eternity to gain a toy? For one sweet grape, who would the vine destroy?"
—William Shakespeare

"In the USA, 68% Believe Jesus Christ was the Son of God who came to earth to die for our sins ..."
—Rasmussen Reports @Rasmussen Poll, March 31, 2013

"Great spirits have always encountered violent opposition from mediocre minds."
—Albert Einstein

"Freedom of religion does not mean freedom FROM religion!"
—President Ronald Reagan

In conclusion, I would remind you that even though there are many reasons why individuals become atheists, my clients who never experienced love don't believe true love even exists at all. Those deprived of fatherly love often became atheists—until healed. Atheists think they have reasoned their way to atheism—which is far from the truth. When we think we know more than we really do, our mediocre minds block great insights we could gain from our own spirits and God's Spirit.

It's good to be a thinker, but sometimes we think too much, losing touch with our emotional and spiritual selves, and with God's Spirit. Our unconscious makes about 80 percent of our choices for us! If you believe Webster's Dictionary could all fall together by an explosion in a printing factory, you are capable of "reasoning" your way into becoming an atheist.

Even Josephus, the historian/scholar of Jesus Day, and Jewish, recorded the facts and evidence of the miraculous resurrection of Jesus. If you believe what you like in the Gospel, and reject what you don't like, it is not the Gospel you believe, but yourself.

Another proof that Christianity is true is the millions of totally transformed lives in those who have put their faith in Jesus. Bill Hybels has said, "There is no thrill in this world better than watching God transform a human life!"

CHAPTER TWENTY-SIX

My Four-Fold Daily Prayer

Prayer and Scripture Meditation Time

Daily prayer and meditation are a must if you desire to grow in wisdom and in your relationship with God outside the box. We learn in Proverbs 3:19-24 (King James Version):

"[19] By wisdom the Lord laid the earth's foundations, by understanding he set the heavens in place; [20] by his knowledge the watery depths were divided, and the clouds let drop the dew. [21] My son, do not let wisdom and understanding out of your sight, preserve sound judgment and discretion; [22] they will be life for you, an ornament to grace your neck. [23] Then you will go on your way in safety, and your foot will not stumble. [24] When you lie down, you will not be afraid; when you lie down, your sleep will be sweet."

I personally would never have a specific prayer time for a specific number of minutes or read a specific amount of the Bible daily—that would be too rote for me. Other believers do prefer these things, and have disciplined themselves spiritually in this manner. I have meditated on Scripture almost every day since age 10, but various amounts at impromptu times of day—they are simply a delight. For most of my years, when a passage of Scripture really stands out to me, I jot it down on a small card and carry it in my pocket to review, and often to memorize.

I sin in my acts or thoughts or unconscious motives or neglects every day of my life, like we all do, but my special verses help pull me back in. "Be still and know that I am God (Psalm 46:10)." We think of prayer as ourselves talking to God, but being still and listening is also great. God says our prayers are a sweet aroma in his nostrils.

Sometimes I float on my back all alone, in a hot tub, mingling my prayers with steam. Our experience with the authority figures we had growing up prejudices us against God. Instead of assuming he is hearing our prayers, we may pray things like, "Hey, God, would you mind speaking up a little louder? I have a hard time hearing you sometimes because I don't listen well enough. Thanks."

I heard a wise physician say that there is no such thing as insomnia, only special times of prayer. Of course, there is such a thing as insomnia, but the principle he taught is still very wise for consideration. When I wake up in the middle of the night occasionally and have trouble falling back asleep, I remember what he said and pray until I sleep, and I have learned a lot from those special times of prayer. Worrying too much keeps us from falling asleep on time. Prayer at night before going to sleep, "giving God the night shift," will help us to worry less and sleep better.

On November 15, 1989, I was driving my car home from work while listening, as I usually did, to the Bible on a cassette tape in my car. I just "happened" to be on Psalm 66 and vaguely remember hearing words like men flying over my head but God delivering me from the fire and from the water. "What a strange passage," I thought to myself as I made a left turn at a major intersection.

I was so distracted that I drove head on into an incoming car, both of us going about 40 miles an hour. My car flipped high into the air and turned around front to back, flipping and landing directly with my roof on the pavement. The other people in other cars around me were literally flying over my head, so to speak. Both cars were totaled, and my front end was destroyed, but God delivered me from the fire and water spewing from the front of my car. My car was squished in everywhere except where I sat, as I hung upside down from the seatbelt that saved my life.

I broke the front window with my elbow and loosened the seatbelt so I could crawl out of the car before it caught fire. As I was flying in the air before landing upside down, I was at total peace, thinking "Oh, this is what God has in store for me today." But when I crawled out of my car, even though the driver of the other car and myself were both unscratched, I was suddenly filled with delayed fear.

But I still foolishly took the risk of crawling back into my upside-down car to get the cassette tape and my *Dallas Cowboy Weekly* magazine, which I also read devotionally as a habit (LOL). A family who witnessed the accident called 911 and the ambulance came before the police arrived. The ambulance driver, seeing neither driver had a scratch, was driving off as the policeman arrived. The policeman saw me standing in my suit next to my car and assumed I was a bystander. He assumed the driver of my car must have died and asked me if the ambulance driver had just taken off with the body.

"I am the body," I assured him, and he was astonished that I was unscratched.

That night I had one of my many "God dreams"—dreams in which Jesus appears and tells me specific things that come true the next day. Jesus told me in the dream to wake up, get the cassette tape, and listen to it in my Walkman until I heard a verse that "knocked me between the eyes." I started where I had left off, with Psalm 66. I listened on and on, and it was 3 a.m., so I asked Jesus to please hurry and give me the right verse. But it took awhile, and finally Jesus "knocked me between the eyes" with Psalm 90:12: "Teach us to number our days, that we may gain a heart of wisdom (NIV)." What God showed me from that verse is that he wanted me to pretend like I died in that accident. Statistically, I should have. And now each day, ever since, when I wake up, I begin my new day realizing that this day is a gift from God, a bonus day that I do not deserve.

The morning after the accident, I called my mother-in-law to tell her I had had an accident. She was only a little surprised about it, and informed me that she had been praying every day for one week now that I and her other sons and daughters and their mates would not die in a car accident that day.

I could hardly believe her, but I know her to be an honest and godly woman. So I asked her why she would pray such an unusual prayer. She shocked me again by saying that the week before, she went to bed meditating on Psalm 90:12, "Teach us to number our days ..." and that she had a conviction that one of her children was going to get into a serious car accident, so she didn't tell any of us about it, but prayed for us individually by name every day since that verse stood out to her and led her to develop that peculiar fear.

It was my sign from God that my God dream the night before was indeed a God dream. I had a dream like that once about my own daughter stopping suddenly on a highway and being rear-ended, so my wife and I prayed for her safety that day, and that very afternoon she called us from California to inform us that she was driving down a California highway at 70 miles per hour when her brakes suddenly locked and an illegal alien in the car behind her ran into the rear of her car but no one was hurt. I believe we all have many so-called "coincidences" in our lives that are actually God intervening in secret ways that we usually overlook, so keep your eyes open for events like this in your own life that you may be missing.

Be aware of God around you, as Psalm 139 says, hugging you with one arm and leading you with the other.

As a result of my car accident on November 15, 1989, and the subsequent dream and events and meditations that followed, I developed a morning prayer in which I pray for the same four things almost every morning ever since. You will see all four of these incorporated into the guidelines for overcoming and growing from our crises in this book. Here are the four things I pray for every morning:

1. "Dear Lord, help me to become more like you today." Because of this simple prayer, I am able to fix my eyes on Jesus and, when anything goes wrong that day, I can thank God for my crisis of the day because it know it will help me accomplish the very desire I prayed for that very morning—to become more like Jesus. Without crises and disappointments I will not grow very rapidly. I do pray that God will help me to learn as much as possible the easy way. I pray that I will be a good listener, so he won't need to allow as many crises in my life to grow me up.

2. "Lord, help me to serve you today." My goal that day is not for some personal gain, but to be used by God to reach out in love and dance with the world that day in some way that I will be a blessing to at least one other person.

3. "Lord, help me to stay out of trouble today." I know I am a sinner, fully capable of committing sins of omission or commission. But sins all hurt somebody—either God, myself, or others—so I do not really want to sin, but sin is nevertheless so very tempting! The Bible says we have had a sufficient day if we have avoided evil that day and that God enables us to be sufficient, with his help, to handle the evils of the day. I pray each day for God to guard my heart. The "heart" implies our mind, emotions, and will. Because we are human and prone to err, God warns us to guard our hearts (Proverbs 4:23). King Solomon (Proverbs 4:23) advised us to guard our hearts above all else because it will determine the course of our lives.

4. And finally, "Lord, help me to learn and grow from whatever things may go wrong today." I expect to have a normal life, and normal lives all include disappointments, failures at times, and crises at times. I expect to suffer one or more disappointments each day, and most days go by without one, so I consider those days as bonus days.

It gives me a totally different perspective than I had before the accident. I am able to fix my eyes on Jesus and see things from an eternal perspective. Before the accident I would get angry, even with God, when I had disappointments and crises. I would be surprised and even shocked by them, as though I somehow deserved to be crisis free. I was more narcissistic and entitled than I am now, although I still struggle with these attitudes. And I tended to "catastrophize"—to assume the worst scenario when a crisis did arise.

Now I view my life in the perspective of eternity. I expect crises, so every day that goes by without one is a pleasant surprise. When crises do arise, I am not surprised much by them, and I accept them as part of life. I accept them as a challenge to get past with the help of my loving God. I expect them to help me grow not only stronger but closer to God. I also have a better understanding of my own depravity (narcissistic tendencies in psychological terminology).

When I find myself having selfish thoughts I am not surprised by them. I accept my humanity and merely admit them to God, who already knows about them before I even think them anyway. I resist them and they go away. When I do sin I confess my sins to God and to my prayer partner. When I have any problems related to aging, I get that in perspective also.

I reckon myself to have already died on November 15, 1989, during my dramatic car accident, so every day I have lived since then is a bonus day here on earth. I realize I could die today, and that every day I live is a gift from God, even if it is with occasional aches and pains from the aging process. I realize that an important part of life is death, and that the death of God's children is a blessing to him from his perspective. The day of my death will be a good day—a day I begin a perfect eternal life filled with so much joy that we humans are not even capable of imagining it. The Apostle Paul said in Philippians 1:21, "For me to live is Christ, and to die is gain."

Every day here on earth is a day to pursue getting to know God more intimately and more outside the box. My Scripture meditation is spontaneous and varies. God's word is powerful. It will accomplish whatever God wants it to accomplish in you and in me. By age 12, I enjoyed reading the sermons of the famous (now deceased) British pastor Charles Spurgeon. Spurgeon, talking about God's word, said, "The Word of God is like a lion.

You don't have to defend a lion. All you have to do is let it loose and it will defend itself. "

My prayers are also spontaneous and varied but daily—in fact, many times daily, even silent prayers for help during my psychiatric sessions with my clients. My prayers are not formal, but rather friend to friend. The most effective prayer you may ever pray is to "be still before the Lord and wait patiently for him." Insights come from this. In Psalm 37:7, King David teaches us that sometimes it's good to quietly listen to the Lord and wait patiently for God to act on your behalf.

My life on earth, compared to eternity in Heaven, is like a breath of air (hot air sometimes!) that comes and is gone, so let's live to love! I love nice things, but how foolish I am when I am tempted to live for temporary things when God and people will last and love forever?

We must all choose to be one person, as we really are, or two people—our public persona and our true but private self, hiding flaws deceitfully. Pretending to love is not the same as genuinely loving in our true selves. I can only love, respect, and be at peace with myself when my public self and private, secret self merge with each other into the same person. I have wasted way too much time in my life being two people!

Have you ever nearly lost your life? "I have been crucified with Christ; and it is no longer I who live, but Christ lives in me (John 12:32)." As we grow spiritually, we still keep our basic personality, but that true self becomes more like Jesus—capable of loving and being loved more deeply.

If we want to lovingly and honestly be a positive influence, Solomon advises us that "pleasant words are persuasive (Proverbs 16:21)." Positivism and encouragement breed more positivism and encouragement. As normal believers, we are all flawed but hopefully praying, like King David, "Create in me a clean heart, O God. Renew a loyal spirit within me (Psalm 51:10)." In that verse, David doesn't pray for God to keep his heart perfect, but rather, "Create in me a clean heart (and loyal spirit)."

Sanctification is a lifelong process never completed until we get to Heaven. God never runs out of character flaws for us to improve upon. Denominations that teach that their members can be sinless use massive, sinful self-righteousness and deny I John 1 and many other scriptures. As we read in James 3:2, "We all stumble in many ways." But as flawed as we are, we are still significant to God, who says, "I am the LORD, the God of Israel, who summons you by name (Isaiah 45:3)." May the God of Israel, who summons me by name, enable me to obey The Great Commandment by growing in my ability to more intimately love him, others, and myself in a deeply spiritual sense.

Great News

Jesus promised to you and to me, "Here I am! I stand at the door and knock. If anyone hears my voice and opens the door, I will come in (Revelation 3:20)."

What a wonderful parting thought. The true Creator-God of the universe, outside the box, loves each of us individually so much that he is standing this very moment outside your heart's door, knocking. He desires emotional and spiritual intimacy with you more than you could ever desire it from him. But he won't come into your heart unless he is invited. Hear his voice right now. Open your door right now. He will come in this very moment.

Printed in the USA
CPSIA information can be obtained
at www.ICGtesting.com
JSHW021956150824
68134JS00055B/1317